Rome

Jack Altman and
Francesca Grazzi

CITYSCAPE

JPMGUIDES

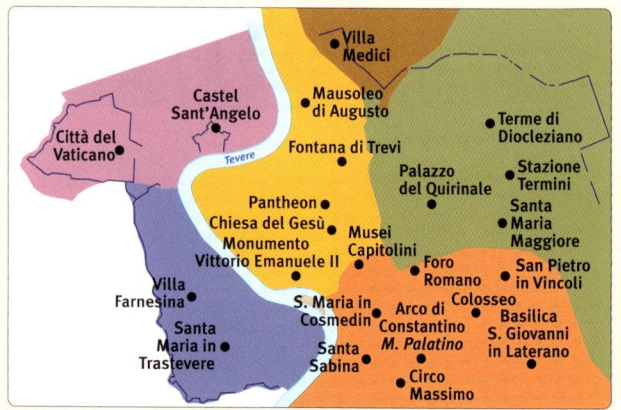

A living open-air museum, Rome offers so much to see that it's best to plan your sightseeing day in advance. We have divided the city into six manageable segments, while visits entailing a trip by metro or train are listed under Excursions.

Contents

Features
Artists Who's Who	12
Spaghetti alla matriciana	37
Shopping	40
Bernini's Rome	52
Rome for Children	70
On the Screen	84

Maps
Centre	96
Around the Quirinale	98
EUR	99
The Vatican	100
Via Appia Antica	102

Fold-out maps
Rome
Metropolitana di Roma

Our favourite sights are marked with a star ★ in the table at the beginning of each section.

cityLights 5
cityPast 9
citySights 17
   Ancient Rome 18
   Historic Centre 28
   Villa Borghese 42
   Quirinal and east of Centre 46
   Trastevere 54
   Vatican Area 58
   Excursions 66
cityBites 73
cityNights 81
cityFacts 87
Index 103

cityLights

Heart of the once mightiest of empires and centre of a universal religion, Rome is almost only incidentally capital of Italy, and only from 1870. The great city, so venerated around the world, is regarded with remarkable disdain by the Italians themselves. The haughty, dynamic Milanese consider it woefully provincial, Florentines feel it lacks dignity, others bemoan its cynicism, a carefully nurtured indifference known as *menefreghismo*. Far from protesting, the Romans, often outrageously easygoing, just laugh. They still have the most enchanting capital in Europe.

Rome is fuelled by government, religion and tourism, and it has always been this way. For the city's non-stop flow of pilgrims and tourists, the business of bread and circuses has been variously operated by emperors and senators, popes and cardinals, or presidents and prime ministers.

Over the ages, it has produced this citizenry of smiling cynics, all knowing that the only way to make their way through a day in the city is through some variation on the *combinazione*.

To get things done, from a place to park the car to an audience at the Vatican or a good seat for the A.S. Roma or Lazio football match, everybody has to know someone somewhere. Even the city's thousands of clergymen and women seem to participate in this supremely Roman art of clever manoeuvring. Witness the skill with which nuns weave their way through the traffic on motor scooters, or the unnerving sight of priests in mirror-lens sunglasses, like celebrities in the grand old Dolce Vita days on the Via Veneto.

Romans can smile because history is on their side. And it is still everywhere you look, despite centuries of wars and devastating city planning, from despotic popes via 19th-century nationalism to modern fascist dictatorship.

Unabashedly Eternal, the city proclaims its attachment to all the great periods of western civilization. Sipping your cappuccino on the Piazza Navona, you may spot a white-clad policeman trying to stop a Ferrari cruising around Bernini's 17th-century fountain on the site of Emperor Domitian's ancient Roman sports stadium. Pillars, arches and carved masonry of pagan temples have been recycled to build baroque churches among the ruins of the Forum. The modern highways leading north, south, east and west out of the city still bear their ancient names—Via Aurelia, Via Appia, Via Flaminia, Via Cassia. St Peter's basilica is built over the tomb of the Apostle martyred here in the 1st century. The Vatican palace and museums combine the glories of Etruscan, Greek and Roman antiquities with the treasures of Renaissance and baroque art—as well as a Salvador Dali Crucifixion and episcopal robes designed by Matisse. Nowhere is the unity of the ages more eloquently expressed than in the spectacle of a Verdi opera at the monumental Baths of Caracalla.

Rome's special relationship with eternity inspired painters, sculptors and architects to produce their greatest works of genius here: Michelangelo's Moses and his frescoes for the Sistine Chapel, Bernini's piazza and baldacchino for St Peter's, Caravaggio's formidable paintings for the churches of San Luigi dei Francesi and Santa Maria del Popolo.

A Place For All Ages

Luckily, not everything in Rome is eternal. The town is also attached with equal enthusiasm to the most ephemeral but no less dazzling tastes of modern fashion. Leading away from the famous Spanish Steps—Piazza di Spagna—the narrow streets of Via Condotti and Via Borgognona are lined with some of the most opulent boutiques in the world, many of them grandly housed in medieval or Renaissance palaces. More popular "street fashion" is to be found on nearby and noisier Via Tritone and Via del Corso. Lovers of modern art and antiques head for Via Margutta and Via del Babuino.

The Spanish Steps area is a microcosm of Rome's appeal to all ages. The young crowd hangs out on the steps themselves, elderly aunts congregate at Babington's genteel tea rooms and sophisticated lovers arrange a rendezvous in the more discreet corners of the elegant old Caffè Greco.

The City of Nine Hills

The site chosen for Rome was ideal: relatively sheltered on the coastal plain, centrally situated on a peninsula, with easy access to the sea via the Tiber river for conquest of the Mediterranean. For the magic of numbers, the city has always claimed to be built on seven hills. Building, rebuilding, landfill and earthquakes have reshaped and flattened out the hillocks that in any case never rose higher than 50 m (164 ft) above sea level.

On the east bank of the Tiber, crowned by Michelangelo's Piazza Campidoglio, the Capitoline hill is the site of the ancient Roman Capitol—and today's city hall. Immediately to the south, above the Forum, is the Palatine hill where legend says the city was founded on the precise date of April 21, 753 BC.

North of the Capitoline is the Quirinal, which lends its name to the Italian president's palace, while the neighbouring Viminal hill has completely disappeared. On the Esquiline to the east, now more plateau than hill, stands the church of Santa Maria Maggiore, while the park of Celimontana is the main feature of the Celian hill.

On the southern outskirts of the old city, away from the bustle of traffic, is the Aventine, a revered sanctuary in ancient times and now a serene and pleasant residential district.

Across the Tiber, two other hills raise the number to nine—the Janiculum, with its fine park, and finally the state within the city, the Vatican, where a thousand people live and work.

cityPast

Legends often have at least one foot in real history. One such is the famous story of Rome being founded on the Palatine Hill in 753 BC by the twin sons of Mars, Romulus and Remus, who were suckled in a cave by a shewolf. Archaeologists seem to agree that the mid-8th century BC is a very likely date for the emergence of the first identifiable Roman township. This would have been a consolidation of several settlements built on the Palatine, Capitoline and Aventine hills to escape the malarial swamps down by the Tiber. The east bank at the river bend of the modern city centre had been settled with Bronze Age cabins since around 1500 BC.

The twins may also be taken as a dual metaphor for the Italic shepherds and farmers (Romulus) and the more sophisticated Etruscan merchants and craftsmen (Remus). Romulus later killed his brother, just as the Italic tribes of Latins and Sabines absorbed, dominated and ultimately eliminated the Etruscan civilization. It was the Etruscan kings who, from the 7th century BC, built the city walls, the Cloaca Maxima sewers to drain the marshlands and the Circus Maximus to entertain the people.

In 509 BC, the Romans overthrew the last of their Etruscan monarchs, Tarquinius Superbus, and established an aristocratic Republic. Over the next 400 years, the governing patricians were constantly at loggerheads with a litigious class of plebeians. The latter elected tribunes to represent them in courts of law in order to settle land disputes, and also to guarantee a regular supply of grain for their daily bread. More disturbingly, the few wealthy plebeians sought social and political equality.

Glories and Horrors of Empire

Apart from the temporary setback of an invasion by the Gauls in 390 BC, Rome progressively overwhelmed the entire Italian peninsula and began to conquer its Mediterranean neighbours. The aristocratic class held on to the spoils of victory and assassinated any recalcitrant champions of the people, such as the Gracchus brothers (in 134 and 123 BC). From civil war emerged another conquering hero, Julius Caesar. His popular dictatorship threatened to upset the delicate balance of patrician power until 44 BC, when he, too, was assassinated.

For the next 17 years, his adopted son had to fight off his rivals Brutus and Mark Antony to claim the title of Rome's first emperor. Augustus Caesar laid the foundations of Rome as the imperial capital of which we can now see the monumental remains—the Forum, temples, senate house, public baths and theatres.

After the crucifixion of Jesus, Jewish and Christian refugees and slaves were deported to Rome. In AD 64, Nero accused Christian revolutionaries of setting fire to the city and had apostles Peter and Paul executed. More constructively, but no less bloodthirstly, Emperor Vespasian had the Colosseum built for gladiator contests. Titus erected a triumphal arch to celebrate his destruction of Jerusalem, while Trajan commemorated victories in the Balkans with a column. Hadrian, the most creative of all the emperor-builders, contributed the magnificent Pantheon, as well as his family mausoleum, today known as the Castel Sant' Angelo. After a chequered history, it has been reconverted into the National Museum.

If Augustus set the tone of the empire's first century as the great age of building, the second was distinguished by philosopher Marcus Aurelius as an era of enlightenment. He improved living conditions for the poor, eased the cruelty of penal law and clamped down on the vicious brutality of gladiators. But Christians, an ever-growing threat to his empire, continued to be persecuted.

Decline began in the 3rd century, when military commanders waged constant power struggles in outposts of northern Europe and Asia. A succession of coups d'état brought no fewer than 25 emperors within 75 years.

Christians and Barbarians

Emperor Constantine (306–337) saw the apparently inexorable growth of Christianity as a useful means of strengthening his beleaguered hold on the empire. He espoused their cause (though converting only on his deathbed) and moved his capital in 330 to Byzantium, subsequently called Constantinople (and now Istanbul). Before the resultant split into eastern and western empires, Rome's own Christian foundation was ensured with the building of a host of churches, notably San Giovanni in Laterano and St Peter's basilica.

As the new Byzantine capital prospered, Rome was plunged into a dark age of pillage and destruction. Invasions of Goths and Visigoths, Vandals and Ostrogoths swept through the city from 410. The population had dwindled from a high point of more than a million under Marcus Aurelius to a mere 50,000 by the time the Germanic conqueror, Odoacer, arrived in 476. He deposed the city's last emperor, Romulus Augustulus (Little Augustus), so named because he was a mere boy when his father put him on the throne.

HISTORY AND MYSTERY

Two modern authors have chosen Ancient Rome as the setting for entertaining whodunnits. American writer Steven Saylor's private investigator Gordianus the Finder gets embroiled in all kinds of racy adventures in *Roman Blood, Arms of Nemesis*, and so on (novels and short stories). Marcus Didius Falco, the lovable sleuth dreamed up by prolific British writer Lindsey Davis, spends most of his time getting into and out of trouble in Rome and various parts of the Roman Empire in *The Silver Pigs* (set largely in Britain), *Shadows in Bronze, Venus in Copper, Time to Depart*, and more. Essential reading for your trip.

ARTISTS WHO'S WHO

A short list to help you find your way among the galaxy of Italian painters and sculptors whose works you'll see in Rome. They often have *given names* (sometimes different in English).

- Andrea d'Agnolo, known as *Andrea del Sarto*, 1486–1531
- Giovanni Battista Gaulli, known as *il Baciccia* or *Baciccio*, 1639–1709
- Donato di Angelo, known as *Bramante*, 1444–1514
- Francesco Castelli, known as *Borromini*, 1599–1667
- Michelangelo Merisi or Amerighi, known as *Caravaggio*, c.1571–1610
- Annibale *Carracci*, 1560–1609
- Domenico Zampieri, known as *il Domenichino*, 1581–1641
- Guido di Pietro, Fra Giovanni da Fiesole, *il Beato* or *Fra Angelico*, 1387–1455
- Giovanni Francesco Barbieri, known as *il Guercino*, 1591–1666
- Michelangelo Buonarroti, generally just *Michelangelo*, 1475–1564
- Jacopo Negretti, known as *Palma il Vecchio* (Old Palma), c.1480–1528. *Palma il Giovane* (the Younger) is his brother's grandson (1544–1628).
- Francesco Mazzola, *il Parmigianino*, 1503–1540
- Bernardino di Betto, *il Pinturicchio* ("the dauber"), 1454–1513
- *Raffaello* Sanzio (Raphael), 1483–1520
- Antonio Cordiani da *Sangallo il Giovane* (the Younger), 1483–1546
- *Tiziano* Vecellio (Titian), 1490–1576
- Jacopo Comin or Robusti, known as *il Tintoretto*, 1518–1594

Michelangelo, Sistine Chapel

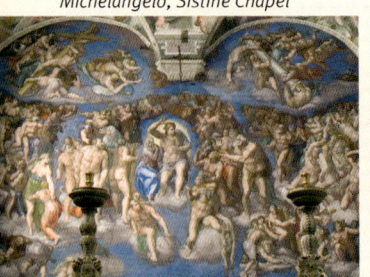

Carracci, Assumption of the Virgin

Quick work by Pope Leo I a few years earlier put the church on a sounder footing than the city itself. He talked the Huns into bypassing Rome and the Vandals out of putting the entire populace to the sword. On Christmas Day, 800, Charlemagne reinforced the pope's position by having himself crowned emperor in St Peter's basilica.

More violence was to follow. When it was not civil war among local aristocrats, it was foreign attacks—the Arabs in 846, Normans in 1084—and a whole string of papal and imperial armies from inside and outside Italy, until the pope fled to Avignon in 1309. Blood continued to flow in pitched battles between the aristocrats and the populist republicans of tribune Cola di Rienzo.

Renaissance and Church Militant

After Gregory XI decided to end the "Babylonian captivity" and return to Rome in 1376, papal leadership was restored in the city with a new vigour. During the 15th and 16th centuries, despite suspicious murmurs of libertarian individualism, successive popes encouraged the flowering of the Renaissance in the sciences and above all in the arts. St Peter's basilica was completely rebuilt, and every pope added splendid apartments to the Vatican palace. The Vatican Library was founded by scholarly Nicolas V; Julius II, the dynamic warrior pope, called in Michelangelo to paint the ceiling of the Sistine Chapel; while his Medici successor, Leo X, commissioned Raphael and master builder Bramante. Rome recaptured the grandeur of its ancient imperial days, infused with a new spirit of humanism.

Inevitably, with the opulence came corruption and more violence. The armies of Emperor Charles V sacked the city in 1527. The even greater threat of Martin Luther's Protestant Reformation had to be opposed by a tough movement to reassert the authority of the Catholic church. The counter-attack was led by the newly founded Jesuits, who promoted the forceful style of baroque architecture, exemplified by Bernini, as well as emphatically Christian themes in painting and sculpture. Protestants left the city and fled north to Switzerland. For the first time, Rome's Jews were confined to a ghetto. The Inquisition weighed in against heretics, philosopher Giordano Bruno was burned alive and Galileo forced to deny his scientific findings.

Capital of Italy

As the 18th century rolled towards revolution, the conservative Austrian Habsburgs took command in Italy, and the papacy was stripped of all real power. When the armies of the French Revolution marched in to proclaim a Roman Republic in 1798, Rome offered no resistance. Napoleon Bonaparte's conquest brought a new sense of nationhood to Italy and, after his defeat in 1814, Rome was the natural choice for a future capital. Backed by Giuseppe Garibaldi's fiery Risorgimento army, national patriot Giuseppe Mazzini declared a new republic in 1848, forcing Pope Pius IX to flee. He returned six months later, under the protection of Napoleon III's French troops. The Italian kingdom was finally established in 1862, but minus papal Rome, until Napoleon III's abdication eight years later enabled national troops to capture the city. The pope was again forced into exile, this time to the Vatican, just across the river from the Quirinal palace. In Rome, united Italy at last had a real capital.

Nationalism

The initial spirit of 19th-century nationalism in Rome was one of idealistic independence. By the time the white marble monument to King Vittorio Emanuele II was inaugurated on Piazza Venezia in 1911, this monstrous symbol of the new Italian nationhood exemplified the climate of aggressive jingoism. Its spirit anticipated Italy's enthusiasm for World War I and the advent of the Fascists. After Benito Mussolini led their March on Rome in 1922, King Vittorio Emanuele III made him prime minister, a post that soon turned into a dictatorship.

Il Duce, as Mussolini liked to be known, embarked on the ruthless destruction of historic neighbourhoods to make way for his bombastic new building programmes. It was only natural for the man who regarded himself as the direct heir of the greatest Roman emperors to build the Mussolini Forum, a sports complex now known as Foro Italico. He was ousted in 1943 and shot by Italian partisans two years later.

During the Mussolini era, the Lateran Treaty of 1929 proclaimed Catholicism as the state religion and made the Vatican a sovereign state. Cardinal Eugenio Pacelli, who negotiated the concordat with Nazi Germany, became Pope Pius XII in 1939 and was attacked for his passive attitude to persecution of the Jews during the German Occupation in 1943 (the Vatican officially apologized in 1998). Declared an open city, Rome escaped relatively unscathed from wartime bombing and was liberated in 1944.

Dolce Vita

Post-war Rome epitomized the lighter side of Italy's economic recovery. Federico Fellini celebrated the new frivolity of the early 1960s with his film *La Dolce Vita,* in which he portrayed celebrities and hangers-on in the café society of the Via Veneto. Things darkened in the 1970s with terrorist bombings and kidnappings by Neo-Fascists and the extreme left-wing Red Brigade.

At the dawn of the new millennium, Rome celebrated its Jubilee amid great rejoicing. The monuments were given a facelift and many special events organized for the millions of visitors. But its political soul still appears to be fought over by Mafia moneylaunderers, media magnates and crusading magistrates. Ordinary Romans remain aloof, mainly preoccupied with finding a place to park the car.

citySights

Ancient Rome *From Piazza Campidoglio to the Appian Way*	18
Historic Centre *The area enclosed within the bend of the Tiber*	28
Villa Borghese *Museums and gardens*	42
Quirinal and east of Centre *Around the highest of Rome's seven hills*	46
Trastevere *Since ancient times, the neighbourhood of workers and craftsmen*	54
Vatican Area *A city within the city*	58
Excursions *The suburbs, and away to the hills and beaches*	66

ANCIENT ROME

This chapter explores the classical city, from the cluttered remains of the Forum and Colosseum to the peaceful Appian Way, over whose paving stones Roman legions marched on their way to Brindisi to set sail for the Levant and North Africa.

THE DISTRICT AT A GLANCE

SIGHTS

Architecture
Piazza del Campidoglio ★ 18
Piazza dei Cavalieri di Malta 21

Ancient sites
Foro Romano ★ 20
Fori Imperiali 20
Monte Palatino 20
Colosseo ★ 21
Domus Aurea...........22
Case Romane del Celio 24
Terme di Caracalla ★ 24
Mura Aureliane 24
Via Appia Antica 25
Catacombe 25
Villa dei Quintili 25

Churches
Santa Maria in Cosmedin 21
Santa Sabina 21
San Pietro in Vincoli .23
San Clemente 23
San Giovanni in Laterano...................23

Greenery
Parco del Celio..........24

Monuments
Colonna Traiana ★ 19
Arco di Costantino ...22

Museums
Musei Capitolini.......18

WALKING TOUR 26

WINING AND DINING 74

Piazza del Campidoglio (E4) Michelangelo designed this beautiful trapezoidal square on the top of the Capitoline, as well as the Cordonata, the great stairway leading down to Via del Teatro di Marcello. He also drew the plans for the Palazzo Nuovo and was responsible for the renovation of the façades of the Palazzo dei Conservatori and the Palazzo Senatorio (Town Hall).

Musei Capitolini (E4) The extensive collections of the magnificent Capitoline Museums (the oldest in the world) are shared between the Palazzo Nuovo, which is principally consecrated to sculpture, and the Palazzo dei Conservatori opposite. Here, on the first floor, classical pieces are displayed in the original

The colossal statue of Constantine originally loomed over the Forum.

16th and 17th century décor. You will see the famous Capitoline She-Wolf from the 5th century BC (the twins were added during the Renaissance), and the charming Spinario, of uncertain date, depicting a boy seated on a rock and removing a thorn from his foot. The picture gallery on the second floor displays canvases by masters such as Caravaggio, Guercino, Pier Francesco Mola and Titian. There is also a collection of porcelain. The courtyard was chosen to display the huge "spare parts"—a head, a foot and a forearm—from a colossal statue of Constantine, as big as a four-storey building, discovered in 1487 in the Basilica of Maxentius in the Roman Forum. • **Daily (except Mon) 9am–8pm** (last entry 1 hour before closing). The splendid panoramic terrace of the Caffè Capitolino opens the same hours as the museums. • Piazza del Campidoglio

Colonna Traiana (F4) One of the few ancient monuments which are still almost intact, Trajan's Column is 40 m (131 ft) high. Decorated with a spiral bas-relief, originally painted in bright colours, it illustrates scenes from the wars against the Dacians. Tiny windows throw a faint light onto an interior spiral staircase which climbs to the top (closed to the public). • Via dei Fori Imperiali

Foro Romano (F4–5) Before the Roman Forum could be built, the marshland chosen for its site below the Quirinal, Viminal, Palatine and Capitoline hills had to be drained. The Cloaca Maxima (Great Drain), begun by Tarquinius Priscus in about 600 BC, is still in operation! (It empties into the Tiber near the Ponte Palatino.) The Forum was the market place. Archaeological excavations started in the 18th century are still under way. The view of the ensemble from the top of the Campodoglio is magnificent: you can see the Via Sacra which crosses the Forum and was once the route taken by triumphal and religious processions. Among all the temples, columns, basilicas, arches, public baths, rostra and ancient palaces, note the Arch of Titus and the remains of the grandiose Basilica of Maxentius and Constantine, richly decorated in marble and bronze. • **Daily 9 am to an hour before sunset** • **Entrances: Largo Romolo e Remo, Piazza Santa Maria Novella 53**

Fori Imperiali (F4) When the demands of public life outgrew the Roman Forum, the emperors built other Fora, all in the same area. In the centre of the Julian Forum (54–46 BC), there is a temple to Venus Genetrix (Tempio di Venere Genitrice) and the vestiges of the Basilica Argentaria. There followed the Forum Augusti (31–2 BC), then the Forum Vespasiani (AD 69–75). Domitian began yet another Forum which was completed by Nerva in AD 97. The last to be built, and the best-preserved, was the Forum Traiani (AD 107–113), a masterpiece by the architect Apollodorus of Damascus, financed with booty captured from the Dacians (from a region roughly corresponding to today's Romania). • **Guided tours (in Italian) Sun 11am; Wed, Sat, Sun (in English) 3pm. Visits with audio-guides: Fora Traiani and Augusto Tues, Sun 10am–noon; Fori di Cesare and Nervia: Fri, Sat, Sun 10–10.50am and 3–3.50pm.** • **Via dei Fori Imperiali**

Monte Palatino (F5) According to legend, it was on Palatine Hill that Romulus and Remus were suckled by a she-wolf; a grotto, decorated with mosaics and shells, was discovered in 2007 and is thought to be the Lupercale, related with this foundation myth. The pine-clad hill is one of Rome's most attractive archaeological sites. The splendid Farnese Gardens (*Orti Farnesiani*) nearby are open to the public. From their palaces on the Palatine Hill, the emperors governed a world stretching from the Atlantic to the Euphrates, from the Sahara to the Danube. There's a lot to see here, notably the emperor's private residence, Domus Augustana, the Domus Flavia and the house of Livia. • **Same hours as Foro Romano** • **Piazza Santa Maria Nova 53; access through Foro Romano**

Santa Maria in Cosmedin (E5) Founded in the 6th century, much rebuilt and restored, this beautiful, simple church served the Greek community. It houses some magnificent mosaics and other works of art such as the Bishop's Throne and the Gothic baldaquin of the high altar. Under the porch is the Bocca della Verità, a thick disc of marble sculpted with a face, probably a well-cover dating from the 4th century BC. Tradition has it that this "Mouth of Truth" would bite the hand of a liar: to test the fidelity of a spouse it was enough to place his or her hand in the mouth. In the square in front of the church stand an ancient circular temple of Hercules, a rectangular temple of Portunus, and the 4th-century Arch of Janus. Behind the church are the remains of the Circo Massimo (hippodrome), now a park. • **Daily 9am–1pm, 3–6pm** • **Piazza della Bocca della Verità**

Santa Sabina (E6) Restoration work undertaken in 1914 returned this early Christian church to its primitive simplicity. Light from 9th-century windows illuminates the white Corinthian columns. The carved 5th-century cedar wood doors have 18 panels illustrating scenes from the Bible. • **Daily 6.30am–12.45pm, 3–7pm** • **Piazza Pietro d'Illiria 1**

Piazza dei Cavalieri di Malta (E6) Dedicated to the Knights of the Order of Malta, the square was designed by Piranesi in 1765. Look through the keyhole in the green door of No. 3 and you will see the dome of St Peter's, framed by an avenue of cypresses.

Colosseo (F–G5) Emperor Vespasian chose the site of Nero's private lake for the Colosseum, destined for the entertainment of the populace. Its inauguration by Titus in AD 80 was marked by a celebration which lasted for 100 days, during which 5,000 wild beasts were slaughtered. Of elegant design, the building had 80 arcades leading to a system of staircases, the *vomitoria*, which provided the

In the Colosseum, feral cats roam the ancient stones where lions roared centuries ago.

55,000 spectators with easy access to their seats. • Daily 9am–4.30pm in winter, 9am–7.30pm in summer • Piazza del Colosseo, entrance near Arco di Costantino

Arco di Costantino (F5) The Arch of Constantine is the largest and best-preserved of the ancient Roman triumphal arches. It was built by the Senate and people to celebrate the victory of Emperor Constantine over Maxentius in AD 312. The friezes and reliefs were taken from earlier monuments built during the reigns of Domitian, Hadrian, Trajan and Marcus Aurelius. • **Piazza del Colosseo**

Domus Aurea (G5) Nero's splendid villa, the Golden House, was built in AD 64, after a fire destroyed the city. It used to face a lake surrounded by vineyards, and the entire façade was gilded. After Nero's death, Vespasian had the lake drained to build the Colosseum in its place. The upper storeys of the

villa were razed to make way for Trajan's Baths. The rooms below ground level were discovered during the Renaissance, and some of the grand frescoed halls, painted to resemble grottoes, are thought to have inspired the "grotesque" style used by Raphael and his contemporaries. Part of the decoration of the vaulted nymphaeum is intact. The villa is only partially open after flood damage.
• Tues–Fri, reservation only, ☎ 06 3996 7700 • Via della Domus Aurea

San Pietro in Vincoli (G4) Beneath the altar of this famous church, north of the Colosseum, are the chains from Jerusalem and Rome which bound the imprisoned Saint Peter. Legend has it that when the two were put in contact, the links miraculously welded together. The church is chiefly known for the tomb of Julius II, a masterpiece by Michelangelo, even though it falls short of his original design which envisaged no less than 40 statues. Before beginning to work, Michelangelo spent eight months at Carrara searching for perfect blocks of marble. Only after several years, in 1513, did he succeed in completing three statues, that of Moses and those of Jacob's wives, Rachel and Leah. Look particularly at the hands of Moses; you can almost see the blood coursing through the veins. He bears horns, the result of a mistranslation in the Vulgate of the Hebrew for "light". • Daily 7am–12.30pm, 3.30–6pm • Piazza di San Pietro in Vincoli 4A

San Clemente (G5) East of the Colosseum, the basilica is made up of three superimposed buildings. In the upper church (12th-century) note the handsome marble paving, and the glittering mosaic in the apse representing the Triumph of the Cross. From the sacristy, stairs descend to the 4th century basilica adorned with faded Roman frescoes. From the nave, ancient steps lead down to a network of passages and rooms which were probably Roman houses, and a pagan temple dedicated to the cult of Mithras. • Mon–Sat 9am–12.30pm and 3–6pm; Sun and holidays 10am–6pm. Underground rooms same hours • Via San Giovanni in Laterano

San Giovanni in Laterano (H6) Fifteen statues of Christ and various saints crown the 18th-century façade of St John Lateran, the Cathedral of Rome, built between 313 and 318 on even more ancient foundations. Until 1870, the Popes were crowned here. Today, the Pope celebrates Mass in the cathedral on

Maundy Thursday. The baptistry dates from the reign of Constantine but was given its present octagonal form in 432. The cloister, surrounded by small twisting columns encrusted with mosaics, is exquisite. Opposite the cathedral, on the east side of the square is the Scala Santa, the holy staircase built of 28 steps which Saint Helen brought from Jerusalem. They are believed to be from the staircase which Jesus descended when leaving the palace of Pontius Pilate after his condemnation. Penitents climb it on their knees. • **Daily 7am–7pm, to 6 pm in winter** • Piazza San Giovanni in Laterano

Parco del Celio (F–G5) South of the Colosseum, this is one of Rome's most beautiful green spaces. Quiet and well-maintained, it is ideal for relaxation.

Case romane del Celio (G5–6) On three underground floors beneath the basilica of Santi Giovanni et Paolo, a maze of ancient dwellings comprising 20 rooms dates back to the 2nd century BC. They were joined in the 3rd century to form a large patrician residence, and the basilica was built on top in the 5th century. Many of the rooms are decorated with frescoes, mosaics and marble inlay, all carefully restored. • **Daily except Tues, Wed, 10am–1pm and 3–6pm. Advanced booking required for groups of 15–25. Guided tours by reservation only** ☎ 06 7045 4544 • Santi Giovanni e Paolo, entrance on Via Clivo di Scauro

Terme di Caracalla (map 5, F–G7) These baths (completed in AD 217) could hold 1,500 people. A treatment took place in several stages. After warming-up exercises, the body was oiled and scraped from tip to toe. Then the client entered the *laconicum* to perspire and afterwards took a hot bath in the *calidarium*. After a short rest to cool down in the *tepidarium* and then the *frigidarium*, there came a session in the cold-water swimming pool, the *natatio*. The last stage was a perfumed massage—early aromatherapy! For spiritual renewal there were libraries, art galleries, gardens and terraces serving as a solarium— everything a modern leisure centre can provide. • **Tues–Sun 9am–an hour before sunset; Mon 9 am–1pm** • Viale delle Terme di Caracalla 52

Mura Aureliane (map 5, F8–J1) Begun by the Emperor Aurelius in AD 270, the Aurelian Wall protected the city from attack by Barbarian tribes. Covering a length of 18 km (11 miles), with 18 gates and 381 towers, the ramparts enclose most of the principal historic monuments of the city. Porta di San Sebastiano, a gate southeast of the Baths of Caracalla, has an interesting museum devoted to the wall and the Appian Way. • Daily (except Mon) 9am–7pm • Vantage point at Porta San Sebastiano

Via Appia Antica (map 5, H10–I12) This major road went all the way to Brindisi. It was lined with splendid monuments, of which only a few vestiges remain. The church known as Domine Quo Vadis (Whither goest thou, Lord?), where Saint Peter met Jesus while escaping from Rome, is open during Mass.

Catacombe di San Callisto (map 5, H11) The catacombs of St Calixtus, on four levels, have been partly explored. Frescoes decorate the most important crypts; in that of the Popes, at least 14 Pontiffs are buried. • Daily (except Wed) 9am–noon and 2–5pm. Closed in February. • Via Appia Antica 110

Catacombe di San Sebastiano (map 5, I12) The remains of martyred Saint Sebastian were removed from the crypt beneath the basilica in the 9th century. The walls are covered with graffiti, invocations to Saints Peter and Paul, whose remains may have been hidden here during a period of persecution. • Daily (except Sun) 9am–noon and 2–5pm. Closed mid November to mid December. • Via Appia Antica 136

Catacombe di Domitilla (map 5, H11) The burial place of Saint Flavia Domitilla who converted to Christianity in the 1st century, these catacombs were excavated in the 4th century when the basilica of Saints Nereus and Achilleus was built on the site. They were built on several levels and are decorated with frescoes of classical and Christian scenes. • Daily (except Tues) 9am–noon and 2–5pm. Closed in January. • Via delle Sette Chiese 283

Villa dei Quintili (map 5, inset) The ruins of a splendid rural estate built by two brothers. Emperor Commodus accused them of plotting against him, had them executed and moved into their home, decorating it with loot taken from the homes of other suspected conspirators. • Daily (except Mon) 9am an hour before sunset. Guided tours ☎ 06 3996 7700 • Via Appia Nuova 1092

WALKING TOUR: ROMAN FORUM

The Via dei Fori Imperiali entrance slopes down between the **Tempio di Antonino e Faustina** (left) and the **Basilica Emilia** (right). Turn right to walk west alongside this business district laid out 179 BC, burnt down and rebuilt under Augustus with a granite-columned portico and two-storey brick-walled shops and offices. At the west end, walk right to the **Curia**, the Senate's imposing brick edifice at the time of Julius Caesar. Continue round to the **Arco di Settimio Severo** (triumphal arch of Septimius Severus) erected in 203 to celebrate the emperor's victories in the Middle East, notably the now Kurdish region of Iraq. Beyond the arch, turn left past the orators' open-air platforms of the **Rostri** and look across to the lofty **Colonna di Foca** transported here in 608 to honour Byzantine Emperor Phocas. A paved slope leads up to three Corinthian columns of the **Tempio di Vespasiano** (AD 81). Behind it, the oracular **Portico degli Dei Consenti** (367) was probably Rome's last "pagan" sanctuary. To the left is the 8-column vestibule of the **Tempio di Saturno**.

Double back, turn right, then left, and walk along the **Basilica Giulia** business district built on the Forum's south side under Julius Caesar in 55 BC (when he was away in England) and incomplete at his death. Beyond the Basilica are three Corinthian columns of **Tempio dei Castori** (Castor and Pollux, 484 BC). Beside it, **Santa Maria Antiqua** is the Forum's oldest and most important Christian church (6th century). Past **Tempio di Vesta**, whose circle of columns protected the deity's fire on a marble platform, turn right back at the Tempio di Antonino e Faustina, incorporated in the Baroque church of **San Lorenzo in Miranda**. Continue past the **Tempio del Divo Romolo** (an imperial prince, not one of Rome's founding twins) with a fine bronze door now part of another church, Santi Cosma e Damiano. Beyond it are the massive vaulted halls of **Basilica di Massenzio** whose gilded bronze roofing was used for St Peter's Basilica. Turn right past the Palladian-style church of **Santa Francesca Romana** to end up at the grand **Arco di Tito**, celebrating the destruction of Jerusalem by Emperor Titus.

ANCIENT ROME 27

Explore the hometown ruins of an empire that shaped our world—shops, offices, political and religious monuments, many recycled for the Christian church.

Start:
Foro Romano,
Bus 60 (Via dei Fori Imperiali)

Finish:
Colosseo, Bus 60,
Metro Colosseo

HISTORIC CENTRE

The main street in central Rome is the Via del Corso, stretching for a mile from the Piazza del Popolo to the Piazza Venezia. It is lined with shops, palaces and churches, and is particularly lively at the end of the day, when it is thronged with people enjoying their evening stroll. In this chapter we have included the sights on both sides of the Corso, and the historic centre ringed by the Tiber.

THE DISTRICT AT A GLANCE

SIGHTS

Architecture
Piazza del Popolo 28
Palazzo di Montecitorio............30
Pantheon★ 31
Palazzo Madama 31
Piazza Navona★ 33
Palazzo Farnese 35
Piazza Mattei...........35

Art
Galleria Spada 35
Galleria Doria Pamphilj..................36
Galleria Colonna......36

Atmosphere
Via del Babuino 29
Piazza di Spagna★...30
Campo dei Fiori★ 35

Churches
Santa Maria del Popolo★ 29
Sant'Ivo alla Sapienza 31
San Luigi dei Francesci 32
Santa Maria della Pace......................32
Sant'Agnese in Agone.....................33
Sant'Andrea della Valle 34
San Carlo ai Catinari 35
Chiesa del Gesù........36

Monuments
Fontana di Trevi★ 30
Colonna di Marco Aurelio 30
Pulcino della Minerva...................31

Museums
Museo dell'Ara Pacis 30
Palazzo Altemps.......32
Museo Barracco 34
Crypta Balbi..............36
Museo Nazionale di Palazzo Venezia 36

WALKING TOUR 38

WINING AND DINING 74

Piazza del Popolo (E1) The Porta del Popolo, a triumphal arch pierced in the Aurelian Wall, used to be the entry point for visitors coming from the north: the Latin inscription reads "For a happy and joyful entry, 1655". The arch opens

Neptune surrounded by sea-nymphs on Piazza Navona's Fontana di Nettuno, by Giacomo della Porta.

onto Bernini's lovely oval square, renovated by Giuseppe Valadier (1816–24). The obelisk of Ramses II in the centre once adorned the Circus Maximus. The twin churches of Santa Maria dei Miracoli and Santa Maria di Montesanto guard the entry to the Via del Corso.

Santa Maria del Popolo (E1) There are many works of art inside this church "of the people". The Della Rovere Chapel (right) has a fresco by Pinturicchio (1454–1513); the Cerasi Chapel (to the left of the choir) contains two masterpieces by Caravaggio: *The Crucifixion of Saint Peter* and *The Conversion of Saint Paul*. The Chigi Chapel, the best of all, was designed by Raphael. • Daily 7am–noon and 4–9pm • Piazza del Popolo 12

Via del Babuino (E1) Antique dealers have colonized this street leading from Piazza del Popolo to Piazza di Spagna. A reclining statue of the satyr Silenus, mistaken by early inhabitants for a monkey, gave rise to its name.

Piazza di Spagna (E2) Visitors to Rome are invariably drawn to the travertine steps leading up to the Trinità dei Monti church. It's the perfect place to stop for a rest and bask in the pleasure of being in Rome. The square is named after the Spanish Embassy which stood here in the 17th century. The Fontana della Barcaccia is Bernini's first fountain, designed in collaboration with his father. Look at the prow of the boat to see three bees, the emblem of Pope Urban VIII.

Museo dell'Ara Pacis (E2) The "Altar of Augustan Peace" is an important example of Roman art from the Augustinian period (1st century BC). The Carrara marble altar, now protected from the elements in its own museum, is sculpted with friezes and reliefs depicting Emperor Augustus and his wife Livia, along with priests, magistrates, patricians and gods. It commemorates the peace achieved by Augustus after campaigns in Gaul and Spain, and was rebuilt in 1937–38 from bits and pieces discovered beneath the foundations of the Palazzo Fiano.
• Daily (except Mon) 9am–7pm ☎ 06 8205 9127 • Lungotevere in Augusta

Fontana di Trevi (E3) The Fontana di Trevi, the biggest, most famous, most-photographed fountain (1732–51) in Rome is by Nicola Salvi and represents the ocean. Neptune in the centre is flanked by two Tritons guiding sea horses (the work of Bracci). Filippo della Valle carved the figures in the side niches: *Abundance* on the left and *Salubrity* on the right. Bathing is strictly forbidden, whatever Anita Ekberg did in *La Dolce Vita*. Turn your back to the fountain and throw in a coin—you will be sure to return to Rome. • Piazza Trevi, Via delle Muratte/Via Stamperia

Colonna di Marco Aurelio (E3) The Column of Marcus Aurelius, 30 m (98 ft) high and 3.7 m (12 ft) in diameter, was erected after the death of Marcus Aurelius in AD 180; it commemorates his victories over the barbarians at the Danube frontier. It is built of 28 marble blocks with 20 spiral carvings illustrating his military campaigns. A statue of Saint Paul stands on the top, added in 1589 when the reliefs of the pedestal were removed. • Piazza Colonna

Palazzo di Montecitorio (E3) Built by Pope Innocent X in 1653 after a design by Bernini, this palace was completed in 1697 by Carlo Fontana and became the Vatican Tribunal. The obelisk of Psammetichus (or Psamtik) II which stands in front of the façade was part of the spoils brought from Heliopolis by Augustus. The palace has been the meeting place of the Chamber of Deputies since 1871. • Open 1st Sun of month 10am–6pm (guided tour). • Piazza di Montecitorio

Pantheon (E3) Hadrian built this temple dedicated to all the gods; it became a church in the Middle Ages. The light enters through a single opening, 9 m (30 ft) across, in the centre of the cupola, like an eye in the firmament. Among the Pantheon's treasures are the tombs of several kings of Italy, and that of the painter Raphael. • Mon–Sat 8.30am–7.30pm; Sun 9am–6pm; holidays 9am–1pm • Piazza della Rotonda

Pulcino della Minerva (E3) In 1630, an elephant was brought to Rome; Bernini may have studied it, because his life-size elephant here supporting a 6th-century BC red granite obelisk is perfect apart from an over-long trunk. The monument was erected in 1667 to honour Pope Alexander VII. The Latin inscription says: "Whomsoever sees the images inscribed by the Egyptians in their wisdom, the images borne by this elephant, the strongest of all the animals, may he ponder the following: have strength of character and let profound wisdom be your support". • Piazza della Minerva

Sant'Ivo alla Sapienza (E3) There's nothing run-of-the-mill in this church, recognizable from afar by its helicoidal lantern-light surmounted by a cross. Seen close-up, this construction by Borromini (1643–60) is one of the most dynamic achievements of Roman baroque. The ground plan is based on two superimposed triangles with curved sides forming a Star of David. With white-painted walls, the church is light and airy; the four levels of the dome are decorated with stucco of stars, crowns and hosts of angels. • **Daily 10am–noon** • Corso del Rinascimento 40

Palazzo Madama (D3) Built in the 16th century by the Medici banker family of Florence, the palace took the name of "Madama" Margaret of Austria, the illegitimate daughter of Emperor Charles V, wife of Alessandro dei Medici. The sumptuous baroque façade dates from the 17th century. The palace has served as the seat of the Italian Senate since 1871. • **Open 1st Sat of the month 10am–6pm, guided tour** • Piazza Madama 11

San Luigi dei Francesi (D3) The French national church, completed around 1589, contains the tombs of many distinguished Frenchmen, including the painter Claude Lorrain, directors of the Académie Française, and soldiers fallen during the Roman Republic in 1848 or during the Italian Campaign of 1944–45. In a chapel on the left is a monument raised by Chateaubriand to the memory of Pauline de Beaumont. In the Contarelli Chapel, there are many fine canvases by Caravaggio: *The Calling of Saint Matthew, The Martyrdom of Saint Matthew* (with a self-portrait of Caravaggio among other people, bottom left) and *Saint Matthew and the Angel*, his earliest great religious works. • Daily (except Thurs afternoon) 8am–12.30pm, 3.30–7.30pm • Piazza San Luigi dei Francesi 20

Palazzo Altemps (D3) This superb palace was begun in 1477, but construction was not completed until the end of the 16th century. It housed the collections of antiquities gathered by Cardinal Marcus Psiticus Altemps and his heirs, as well as a great library that has been transferred to the Vatican. The palace now belongs to the State and is part of the Museo Nazionale Romano. Apart from the Egyptian collection and the 16 Altemps sculptures, don't miss the remarkable Ludovisi Boncompagni collection. During the Counter-Reformation, great construction works were carried out in Rome, and whenever statues were excavated, they were put on sale, day by day. Boncompagni snatched up several and had them restored by sculptors such as Bernini—the repair work is clearly indicated. The entire palace is beautifully decorated with baroque paintings: on the first floor, for example, the Sala delle Prospettive Dipinte is adorned with landscapes and hunting scenes observed through windows painted in trompe-l'œil. • Daily (except Mon) 9am–7.45pm, sometimes later in summer • Piazza Sant'Apollinare 44

Santa Maria della Pace (D3) Work began on this church in 1482 at the behest of Pope Sixtus IV to celebrate the end of the war with the Turks. The cloister (1504) is by Bramante. Frescoes by Raphael in the Chigi Chapel on the right depict the four Sybils. Baldassarre Peruzzi painted the frescoes in the Ponzetti Chapel on the left. A new façade, with circular entrance, was added in the 17th century by Pietro de Cortone. • Mon–Sat 10am–noon, 4–6pm; Sun and holidays 10am– noon. • Via della Pace 5

Piazza Navona (D3) On the site of the Stadium of Domitian, this square was designed to be filled with water for nautical entertainment. The Fontana dei Fiumi (Fountain of the Four Rivers) in the centre is by Bernini (1651). Each of the four great figures symbolizes a river representing a continent. Europe is personified by Danube, gesticulating vehemently. Ganges, oar in hand, represents Asia. Nile is hidden under a hood, supposedly to signify the mysterious side of the dark continent. For his depiction of the Americas, in the wild, bearded figure of Rio de la Plata, Bernini seems to have let his imagination run amok: he is staring—some say fearfully—at the nearby church of Sant'Agnese in Agone. The two other fountains, Fontana di Nettuno (Neptune) and Fontana del Moro (Moor) in the square are by Giacomo della Porta and were renovated by Bernini, who designed the central figure of the Moor. The obelisk in the middle of the square comes from the Circus of Maxentius. Domitian had it carved with hieroglyphs showing Egyptian divinities paying their respects to Roman emperors.

Sant'Agnese in Agone (D3) Built between the 8th and 12th centuries on the site of the martyrdom of Saint Agnes, the church took on its present form in 1652, a design by Girolamo and Carlo Rainaldi, modified later by Bernini, Pietro de Cortone and lastly by Francesco Borromini who was responsible for the concave façade, the dome and the campaniles.
- Mon–Sat 5–6.30pm, Sun and holidays 10am–1pm
- Piazza Navona

LAMB TO THE SLAUGHTER

The saint to whom the church Sant'Agnese in Agone, on Piazza Navona, is dedicated, was a 4th-century virgin martyr. The 13-year-old daughter of an aristocratic family was slain for refusing to marry the noble suitor her parents had chosen for her. Her symbol is the lamb and on her feast day, January 21, a pallium vestment made from the wool of a specially blessed lamb is given by the pope to a particularly worthy archbishop. The ritual dates back to the 6th century.

The open-air market on Campo dei Fiori is a delight for all the senses.

Sant'Andrea della Valle (D4) Puccini set the first act of his opera *Tosca* in one of the chapels of this church. It is renowned for its dome, the highest in Rome after St Peter's and, like the façade, the work of Carlo Maderno. Several 17th-century artists contributed to the church's decoration: Borromini for the lantern; Lanfranco for the frescoes of the cupola, the *Glory of Paradise*; Domenico Zampieri for the frescoes of the apse and the pendentives (the triangular spaces between the tops of the columns and the cupola). Inside are fine paintings by Calabrese, Domenichino *(St John the Baptist)* and Mattia Preti *(Crucifixion of St Andrew)*. • Piazza Sant'Andrea della Valle

Museo Barracco (D4) The Piccola Farnesina is an elegant palace housing a prestigious collection of antique sculpture from Babylon, Assyria, Egypt, Greece, Rome and Etruria, gathered in the 19th century by Senator Barracco and moved here in the early 1900s. • Daily (except Mon) 9am–7pm ☎ 06 8205 9127 • Corso Vittorio Emanuele II 166A

Campo dei Fiori (D4) In the centre of the old city, this is Rome's most famous and most picturesque market. The range of shining produce on the stalls is of the highest quality and the displays are as beautiful as still-lifes. The old ghetto is clustered around the *campo*. Look around many goldsmiths' workshops in the area, near the Ponte Sisto and along Via del Pellegrino, Via dei Coronari and Via dell'Orso. • Mon–Sat 7am–1.30pm • Piazza Campo dei Fiori

Palazzo Farnese (D4) Built by Cardinal Alessandro Farnese from 1517, this imposing palace was the inspiration for other princely palaces. Among the architects who worked on it were Sangallo the Younger, Michelangelo and Giacomo della Porta. Today it houses the French Embassy. • Mon, Thurs at 3pm, 4pm and 5pm (closed during summer holidays and Christmas to New Year); 50-min guided tours. Reserve 1–4 months in advance by fax 06 6880 9791 or e-mail visitefarnese@france-italia.it • Piazza Farnese

Galleria Spada (D4) The Spada Palace was built in the 1550s for Cardinal Capo di Ferro and later for the Cardinals Spada, two brothers who commissioned Bernini and Borromini (who designed the trompe-l'œil colonnade in the garden). Great art-lovers, the Spada brothers assembled a magnificent collection of 16th- and 17th-century paintings (including works by Rubens, Dürer, Andrea del Sarto, Titian, Guido Reni and Guercino), classical sculpture and 18th-century furniture. • Daily (except Mon) 8.30am–7.30pm ☎ 06 686 1158 • Palazzo Spada, Piazza Capo di Ferro 13

San Carlo ai Catinari (E4) This church of the order of Barnabites is dedicated to Saint Carlo Borromeo, Archbishop of Milan. The façade in travertine marble was completed in 1638. Paintings and frescoes illustrate the life of the Saint, canonized in 1610. The church houses one of Giovanni Lanfranco's finest works, *The Annunciation*. • Daily 9am–noon, 4–6pm. • Piazza B. Cairoli

Piazza Mattei (E4) All the palaces around the piazza belonged to the Mattei family. One of the most interesting is the Palazzo Mattei de Grove with its collection of marble sculpture in the courtyard. The family ordered the charming Fontana delle Tartarughe (Turtle Fountain, 1581–84) to adorn their square. By Taddeo Landini from a design by Giacomo della Porta, it shows four youths each standing with one foot on a dolphin's head. It remains a mystery as to who was inspired to place four turtles on the edge of the basin a century later.

Crypta Balbi (E4) Fascinating "back stage" area of a theatre built by a retired soldier, Lucius Cornelius Balbus in 13 BC. Part of the Museo Nazionale Romano, it explains in a modern, aesthetic manner the city's urban history • **Daily (except Mon) 9am–7.45pm** ☎ 06 3996 7700 • Via delle Botteghe Oscure 31

Chiesa del Gesù (E4) Begun by Vignola in 1568 and finished by Giacomo della Porta in 1584, this was the first Jesuit church in the city. Financed by Cardinal Alessandro Farnese, the church is plain outside. In the 17th century the interior was enriched by splendid works of art: frescoes of the vault by Giovanni Battista Gaulli (Baciccia); the Altar of Saint Ignatius, incorporating an enormous block of lapis-lazuli; and the rooms of Saint Ignatius with a trompe-l'œil corridor by Andrea Pozzo. • **Daily 6.30am– 12.30pm and 4–7pm** • Piazza del Gesù

Museo Nazionale di Palazzo Venezia (E4) Cardinal Pietro Barbo, the future Pope Paul II, ordered construction of this palace in 1455. It became the property of the state in 1916. Mussolini used it as his headquarters and set up his office in the Sala del Mappamondo, named after a fresco showing the world as it was known in 1495. Magnificent collections of early Renaissance paintings, sculptures, tapestries and ceramics. Opposite, the huge white Monumento Vittorio Emanuele II was inaugurated in 1911. • **Daily (except Mon) 8.30am–7.30pm** ☎ 06 32 810 • Via del Plebiscito 118

Galleria Doria Pamphilj (E3–4) A priceless private collection of 16th–18th-century paintings. Marvellous canvases by Caravaggio, Reni, Raphael, Titian, Velasquez, Vanvitelli. • **Daily (except Thurs) 10am–5pm** ☎ 06 679 7323 • Palazzo Doria Pamphilj, Piazza del Collegio Romano 2

Galleria Colonna (E–F3) Housed in part of the Palazzo Colonna, this is a large private collection of 14th–18th century paintings by Tintoretto, Bronzino, Veronese, Carracci, among others. • **Sat 9am–1pm. Open on other days by request on** ☎ 06 678 4350 (groups of 10 persons minimum) Closed in August. • Palazzo Colonna, Piazza SS Apostoli 66

SPAGHETTI ALLA MATRICIANA

Popular in the working-class trattorie of Monteverde and Trastevere, this quintessentially Roman dish prepared with salted pork and tomatoes is typical of the capital's traditional cuisine—simple and no frills. Romans contemptuously dismiss a claim to its invention in Amatrice since a variation of it was being prepared centuries before the little town of northern Lazio even existed. With classical Italian local chauvinism, they add: "Such people have no claim on anything Roman, not even kinship with Pontius Pilate since no man in Amatrice has ever been known to wash his hands." A quite plausible explanation of the name is *matraccio*, a glass flask in which the tomatoes were traditionally preserved. Even today, Romans in the best kitchens prefer to use tinned or bottled rather than fresh skinned tomatoes. For a local wine, connoisseurs suggest a dry red Cesarese del Piglio from Frosinone.

Spaghetti alla matriciana for four
- 20 g lard
- 1 chopped onion
- 125 g salted pork or bacon cut in short strips
- 450 g tomatoes skinned and chopped
- Pepper and salt to taste
- 400 g spaghetti
- Grated *pecorino romano*, a tangy sheep's milk cheese (failing that, Parmesan)

1. Sauté the chopped onion in the lard.
2. Add salted pork or bacon strips to brown for a few minutes.
3. Pour in chopped tomatoes and cook over a high flame, not more than 5 minutes.
4. Cook spaghetti just al dente, strain, place in a hot dish and stir in the well-seasoned sauce.
5. Guests add their own cheese.

WALKING TOUR: HISTORIC CENTRE

North of Piazza Venezia, take **Via del Corso**, one of the city's most popular thoroughfares where horses once raced along the ancient route of Via Flaminia. On the left-hand corner, the Baroque **Palazzo Buonaparte** was the home of Napoleon's mother Letizia after 1815. Beyond it at No.304, the grand **Palazzo Doria Pamphilj** houses a superb art collection (Velázquez, Caravaggio, Bernini), entrance left on narrow Via Lata to **Piazza del Collegio Romano**. The 16th-century Jesuit college founded by Ignatius Loyola, modelled on Paris's Sorbonne, became in the 1930s Rome's first state high school (Liceo Ginnasio). Turn right on Via Sant' Ignazio to the convex and concave façades on the splendid oval **Piazza Sant'Ignazio** with its lovely 17th-century church.

Double back across Piazza San Macuto along Via Seminario past the Jesuit seminary and 16th-century Palazzo Serlupi Crescenzi. Buy an ice cream on **Piazza della Rotonda** and from the steps of the marble fountain (1575), admire Hadrian's **Pantheon**. Right of the Pantheon, take Via della Rotonda and go right on Via della Palombella for an enchanting view of the more modest **Piazza Sant'Eustachio**. Notice to the left, the charming **Palazzetto Tizio da Spoleto** with its 16th-century frescoes, opposite the church with its Romanesque campanile,

Turn right on Via della Dogana Vecchia to the French community's church of **San Luigi dei Francesi**, appreciated less for its ponderous architecture than for Caravaggio's magnificent St Matthew paintings and the Domenichino frescoes inside. South of the church, follow a narrow lane to Corso del Rinascimento and turn left past **Palazzo Madama**, built 1503 by the Medici for Margaret of Austria and now the seat of the Italian Senate. Continue south and at the 16th-century **Palazzo della Sapienza** (once Rome's university and now housing the city archives), take a look across the grandiose courtyard to Borromini's church of **Sant'Ivo**. Cross the street to enter the grand **Piazza Navona** where Emperor Domitian staged his water-shows. Time for another ice cream.

HISTORIC CENTRE

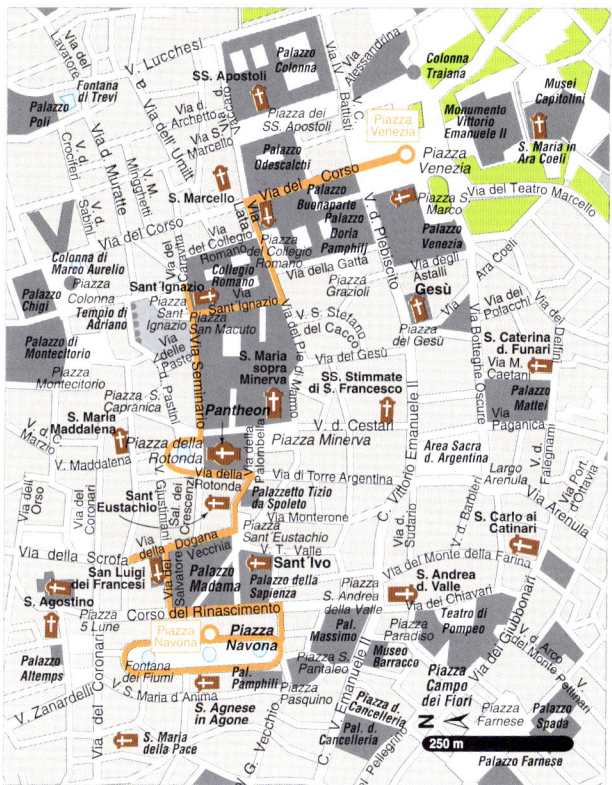

Around the Pantheon, Baroque palazzi and churches stand where the ancient Romans once staged horse races on Via del Corso and fake sea-battles on Piazza Navona.

Start: Via del Corso Bus 60, 64 (Piazza Venezia)

Finish: Piazza Navona Bus 30

SHOPPING

Rome's dazzling array of goods make shopping—and window shopping—as much a feast for the senses as the city's finest museums and galleries. The city's more elegant ladies prefer their goods handmade and shop for them in the magic triangle drawn between Piazza del Popolo, Piazza Navona and Piazza di Spagna.

Italy's top fashion designers can be found in the streets between Piazza di Spagna and Via del Corso. The jewellers *(gioiellerie)* cluster around Piazza di Spagna, while the goldsmiths' workshops are mostly near Campo di Fiori. Leather articles handmade by Italian craftsmen are appreciated the world over. The finest shoes are found in and around Via Condotti. For more moderately priced goods, try the Trevi Fountain area or the markets. Designer boutiques to look out for: **Via del Babuino**: Chanel at No. 98–101 and a branch of Emporio Armani at 140. **Via Bocca di Leone**: Valentino (for ladies) at No. 16 (ladies); Gianni Versace (for ladies) at 27; Mariella Burani at 28. **Via Borgognona**: Dolce & Gabbana at No. 8, Gianni Versace for men at 25; Laura Biagiotti at 43; and several branches of Fendi. **Via Condotti**: Gucci at No. 8; Bulgari at 10; Valentino at 13; Max Mara at 19; Buccellati jewellers at 31, Trussardi at 49; Campanile (expensive shoes) at 58; Furla at 55; Ferragamo's fabulous shops at 64–66 (men) and 73–74 (ladies' clothing and leatherware); Prada at 88. **Via Frattina**: Brighenti at No. 7/8 where the stars buy their lingerie; Max Mara at 28, Testa, for smart young men at 105; Fausto Santini (trendy shoes) at 120–121. **Piazza di Spagna**: Sergio di Cori at No. 53; Dior at 74, Missoni at 77.

Department Stores and Shopping Centres

Despite the Romans' taste for specialized shops, the city has a few department stores.
Most upmarket is **La Rinascente**; the Piazza Colonna branch (E3) was Rome's first

department store (1887), Mon–Sat 10am–9pm, Sun 10.30am–8pm. A bigger store on Piazza Fiume (G1) is open daily 10am–9pm. **COIN**, set in the premises of a former brewery on Via Mantova (H1), just north of Piazzale Porta Pia, is a large-scale department store good for clothing, lingerie, beauty products and perfume, but especially for Italy's superbly designed household goods. A second branch of COIN is behind San Giovanni in Laterano, on Piazzale Appio 7 (off map, dir. H6).

Close to Cinecittà, on Via Tuscolana on the southeastern edge of the city (metro line A), **Centro Commerciale Cinecittà Due** has 100 stores and boutiques, as well as numerous bars, banks and restaurants. Even bigger, at the terminus of metro line B, Laurentina, is **I Granai** shopping centre.

Markets

For local colour, rummage around the city markets. Best known is the **Campo dei Fiori food market** (D4). North of the Vatican, along Via Trionfale (B 1), the wholesale flower market, **Mercato dei Fiori**, is open to the public Tuesday 10.30am–1pm, great for plants and seeds, as well as flowers and many exotic varieties. In the city centre on Largo della Fontanella Borghese (E2), **Mercato delle Stampe**, open Saturday and Sunday 9am–7pm, deals not in stamps but in books and prints. South of the Termini railway station, **Piazza Vittorio Emanuele II** (H4) hosts a large food market, with many other stalls (clothing, pots and pans, leatherware, toiletries), Monday to Saturday 7am–2pm. The Trastevere flea market at **Porta Portese** (D6), Sunday 6.30am–2pm, sells everything from kittens to wardrobes. To get a bargain, you must haggle in Italian. At **Via Sannio**, near San Giovanni in Laterano (H6), along part of the Aurelian Wall, you can buy new and second-hand clothing, and shoes. Open Monday to Friday 8am–1pm; Saturday 8am–6pm.

South of town (off map dir. E6, metro line B to Piramide), the **Mercato di Testaccio** is held Monday to Saturday 6am–1.30pm. The covered part is devoted to food; there are a few clothing stalls outside.

VILLA BORGHESE

The Romans' favourite park is just north of the centre. They come here to cycle, jog, ride horses, play football, to daydream in the shade of the green oaks and umbrella pines, or take a ride in the hot air balloon.

THE DISTRICT AT A GLANCE

SIGHTS

Ancient site
Catacombe di Priscilla 43

Art
Galleria Borghese 42

Galleria Nazionale d'Arte Moderna 43

Greenery
Giardini e Terrazza del Pincio 42

Giardini di Villa Borghese 42

Museums
Museo Borghese ★ ... 42

Museo Nazionale Etrusco di Villa Giulia ★ 43

WALKING TOUR 44

Giardini e Terrazza del Pincio (E1) These magnificent gardens above the Piazza del Popolo were designed by Valadier. The wide, tree-lined alleys are a favourite place for Romans taking a stroll. There's a great view from the terraces. At sunset the dome of St Peter's is bathed in a heavenly golden glow.

Giardini di Villa Borghese (F1) There are several approaches to the gardens of the Villa Borghese: through Porta Pinciana at the end of Via Veneto, from the Giardini del Pincio, or the monumental entrance from Piazzale Flaminio. The huge park was created in 1605 by Cardinal Borghese and became state property in 1902. Within its bounds are museums, galleries, archaeological schools, a zoo, an amphitheatre, an artificial lake, pavilions, fountains, neoclassical statues and fantastic constructions to delight the eye—something for everyone.

Museo e Galleria Borghese (off map, dir. F–G1) On the ground floor of the villa, the museum comprises a picture gallery and an outstanding collection of sculpture, including works by Bernini and Canova. • Daily (except Mon) 9am–7pm. Visits limited to 2 hours; reservation compulsory ☎ 06 32 810
• Villa Borghese, Piazzale Scipione Borghese 5

Galleria Nazionale d'Arte Moderna (off map, dir. E1) Italian painting and sculpture from the 19th and 20th centuries, with works by Carrà, De Chirico, Modigliani, Boccioni, landscape artists from northern Italy, Tuscan impressionists, and so on. One section is devoted to non-Italian artists such as Cézanne, Monet, Klimt, Kandinsky and Utrillo. • Daily (except Mon) 8.30am–7.30 pm ☎ 06 322 981 • Villa Borghese, Viale delle Belle Arti 131

Museo Nazionale Etrusco di Villa Giulia (off map, dir. E 1) Little is known of the Etruscans, a mysterious people who came by sea and settled on the peninsula in about 900 BC. The ancient Romans destroyed all traces of them, but objects exhumed from their burial sites reveal an appealing culture. On display in the Etruscan museum, the biggest in Italy, is the famous Sarcofago degli Sposi (a tomb sculpted like a couch with a reclining married couple), statuettes, gold jewellery and kitchen utensils. • Daily (except Mon) 8.30am–7.30pm ☎ 06 320 1951 • Piazzale di Villa Giulia 9

Catacombe di Priscilla (off map, dir. G 1) A good way out of town in the Villa Ada park, these 2nd-century catacombs are on two levels. They are named after a Roman lady from a family of senators who converted to Christianity in the 1st century. Two painted stuccoes illustrate *The Good Shepherd* and *The Last Supper*. The Greek Chapel is decorated with niches, water features and other ornaments. • Daily (except Mon and all Jan) 8.30am–noon and 2–5pm ☎ 06 8620 6272 • Via Salaria 430 • Bus 135, 235, 319

WALKING TOUR: PIAZZA DI SPAGNA TO PINCIO GARDENS

On the **Piazza di Spagna**, right and left of the stairs leading to Trinità dei Monti, are the **Casina Rossa** where John Keats died in 1821 and **Babington's**, Rome's first and still most famous English tea rooms. Walk around Bernini's **Barcaccia fountain** and leave the piazza by **Via del Babuino** for some high-class window-shopping past antique galleries and luxury boutiques housed in lofty 18th-century mansions. The street takes its name from a baboon-like statue on a fountain, in fact an ancient Roman satyr. Beyond the Via dei Greci is the Greek Catholic church of **Sant'Atanasio** (1583). Detour right and then left to explore the galleries and elegant courtyards of **Via Margutta** before returning to Via del Babuino and the redbrick Anglican Gothic Revival **All Saints Church** (1887). Opposite are two handsome palazzi, **Boncompagni Cerasi** (No. 51) and **Sterbini** (Feltrinelli bookshop, No. 39/40). Further along is the renowned **Hôtel de Russie** (opened in 1822) with its fashionable Stravinskij Bar.

At **Piazza del Popolo** to the left, flanking Via del Corso, are the twin Baroque churches of **Santa Maria in Montesanto** and **Santa Maria dei Miracoli**. The piazza's other twins are the **Caffè Rosati**, historically favoured by leftwing intellectuals, and **Caffè Canova**, frequented by their rightwing counterparts, looking across to the 3,200-year-old Egyptian **Flaminio Obelisk** from Heliopolis.

On the north side of the square, to the right of **Santa Maria del Popolo** (renowned for its Pinturicchio and Caravaggio masterpieces) is the stairway zigzagging up to the **Pincio Gardens** and a magnificent view from Piazzale Napoleone I across the piazza to St Peter's Basilica. Take Viale D'Annunzio along the terrace overlooking the city past **Casino Valadier** (now a café and restaurant). Continue along Viale della Trinità dei Monti past the 16th-century **Villa Medici**, Roman seat since 1804 of the Académie Française. Opposite is the **Caffè Ciampini**, popular for its terrace view of the city. The promenade ends at the **Trinità dei Monti** (1502, one of Rome's many "French" churches, and its stairway leading back down to Piazza di Spagna.

VILLA BORGHESE 45

Walk through one of the city's most fashionable neighbourhoods, two grand piazzas with the greenery of the Pincio Gardens as a bonus.

Start and finish:
Piazza di Spagna Metro, Bus 117, 119

QUIRINAL AND EAST OF CENTRE

This is the modern city of banks, insurance companies, embassies and high-class hotels, spreading from the Via Veneto to the Baths of Diocletian. The Quirinal Hill is the highest of Rome's famous seven; at the top is the residence of the Italian President.

THE DISTRICT AT A GLANCE

SIGHTS

Architecture
Piazza Barberini 46
Piazza del Quirinale ★ 48
Piazza del Cinquecento 49
Piazza della Repubblica 49

Art
Galleria Nazionale d'Arte Antica di Palazzo Barberini 46

Churches
San Carlo alle Quattro Fontane 47
Sant'Andrea al Quirinale ★ 47
Santa Maria Maggiore 48
Santa Prassede 48
Santa Maria degli Angeli e dei Martiri 49

Greenery
Giardini di Villa Aldobrandini 48

Museums
Museo Nazionale delle Paste Alimentari 48
Palazzo Massimo alle Terme 49
Terme di Diocleziano 49

WALKING TOUR 50

WINING AND DINING 77

Piazza Barberini (F2) In the centre of the square stands one of Bernini's most beautiful fountains, the Fontana del Tritone, erected in 1642 for Pope Urban VIII Barberini: four dolphins support a great scallop shell on which a Triton is spouting water through a conch shell. Another lovely fountain by Bernini is hidden in a corner of the same square, at the foot of Via Veneto. The Fontana delle Api is a scallop shell from which three huge bees are drinking.

Galleria Nazionale d'Arte Antica di Palazzo Barberini (F2) Paintings by great European masters of the 13th to 18th centuries are displayed here on one floor, including works by Tintoretto, Holbein (portrait of Henry VIII), Caravaggio *(Judith and Holofernes),* El Greco, Guercino and Raphael *(La Fornarina).* Upstairs

The Fontana delle Api incorporates the bees of the Barberini coat of arms.

are works of the 18th century (Settecento). • **Daily (except Mon) 8.30am–7.30pm; last tickets 30 min before closing.** ☎ 06 32 810, for guided tours ☎ 06 2258 2493 • Via delle Quattro Fontane 13

San Carlo alle Quattro Fontane (F3) This magnificent church designed by Borromini is dedicated to Saint Carlo Borromeo. A riot of curves, it is known as "San Carlino" because of its small size. • **Mon–Fri 10am–1pm and 3–6pm, Sat 10am–1pm, Sun noon–1pm** • Via del Quirinale 23

Sant'Andrea al Quirinale (F3) A Baroque jewel, the elliptical church was designed by Bernini and built by his assistants 1658–70 for the novices of the Society of Jesus. Paintings by Baciccia adorn the chapels. The cupola symbolizes heaven inhabited by cherubs swinging on garlands. The high altar is surrounded by pink marble columns and crowned by a golden cupola where angels cling to heavenly rays of light. • **Daily 8am–noon, 4–7pm** • Via del Quirinale 29

Piazza del Quirinale (F3) The beautiful Fontana di Monte Cavallo enhances the square. Its statues of Castor, Pollux and their horses came from the Baths of Constantine (4th century), while the basin was previously in the Forum and used as a water trough until 1813. The obelisk stood in the Mausoleum of Augustus. The Palazzo del Quirinale (open Sun) is an imposing complex begun in 1730, the work of several great architects including Domenico Fontana, Carlo Maderno and Bernini. First the summer palace of the Popes, then the Royal Palace, it became the official residence of the President of the Republic in 1947.

Museo Nazionale delle Paste Alimentari (F3) A unique museum devoted to pasta in all shapes and sizes, from its hand-rolled origins to modern mass-produced spaghetti. • Daily 9.30am–5.30pm ☎ 06 699 1119 • Piazza Scanderbeg 117

Giardini di Villa Aldobrandini (F4) This state-owned villa is closed to the public but you can wander at will in the gardens, which provide a haven of peace in the city centre, criss-crossed by gravel walks with inviting benches. • Via Mazzarino 1

Santa Maria Maggiore (G3) The different architectural styles of this basilica mingle harmoniously. Inside, the 40 columns and three naves date from the 5th century. Pope Gregory XI had the bell tower constructed on his return from Avignon in 1377. The caisson ceiling was installed during the Renaissance; the two cupolas and the baroque façade are from the 18th century. The site of the church was designated by Pope Liberius, to whom the Virgin Mary appeared in a dream, ordering him to build a church where he found snow. In the middle of a torrid Roman summer, on August 5, 356, it snowed on the Esquiline Hill. Daily 7am–8pm • Piazza di Santa Maria Maggiore

Santa Prassede (G4) Pope Paschal I had the remains of 2,000 martyrs removed from the catacombs and buried here, on the site of a 5th-century church. St Prassede was the daughter of a Roman Senator who gave shelter to Saint Peter. The Chapel of St Zeno in the right-hand nave, covered in golden mosaics, was built on the orders of the same pope as a mausoleum for his mother Theodora. **Daily 7am–noon, 4–6.30pm** • Via Santa Prassede 9A

QUIRINAL AND EAST OF CENTRE

Piazza dei Cinquecento (G–H3) A column of light, the Obelisco di Luce, was erected in the square at the beginning of the year 2000, making a luminous welcome for the millions of millennium visitors arriving at the Termini station.

Palazzo Massimo alle Terme (G2) A Jesuit college built in the 19th century, the palace was carefully restored and opened in 1998 as part of the Museo Nazionale Romano. The ground and first floors are devoted to sculpture. In room VII, look for the Greek Niobide, a young girl trying to pull out an arrow piercing her back. In room V is a pretty crouching Aphrodite. Coins and gold are displayed in the basement, but it is well worth taking the guided tours of the top two floors, where you can see, among other splendours, the dining room *(triclinium)* of Livia's villa (30–20 BC), decorated with frescoes and mosaics, and even more frescoes from a Roman mansion discovered in the Trastevere district when part of the river below the Villa Farnesina was drained. • Daily (except Mon) 9am–7.45pm ☎ 06 3996 7700 • Largo di Villa Peretti 1

Piazza della Repubblica (G2–3) Mario Rutelli created a scandal in 1901 with his Fontana delle Naiadi placed outside the church of Santa Maria degli Angeli. It is adorned with four nude bronze naiads, each reclining on an animal: a water snake representing rivers, a swan symbolizing lakes, a lizard for underground streams and a sea horse for the oceans. In the centre, the sea god Glaucos clasps a dolphin.

Santa Maria degli Angeli e dei Martiri (G2) Incorporated into the ruins of the Baths of Diocletian, this church is dedicated to the angels and the Christian martyrs employed in the building of the baths. Designed by Michelangelo, it was greatly modified by Luigi Vanvitelli in 1749. See the Martyrdom of Saint Sebastian by Zampieri and the statue of Saint Bruno by Jean-Antoine Houdon. Daily 7am–12.30pm and 4–6.30pm, free guided tours in English Tues, Wed, Thurs at 10.30am • Piazza della Repubblica

Terme di Diocleziano (G2) In part of the ruins of the Baths of Diocletian, the Museo Nazionale Romano displays major collections of stucco, frescoes, mosaics and sculpture from various excavations since 1870. • Daily (except Mon) 9am–7.45pm ☎ 06 3996 7700 • Via de Nicola 78

WALKING TOUR: QUIRINAL

On **Piazza Barberini**, start out from Bernini's **Fontana del Tritone** (1643), commissioned by Pope Urbano VIII and bearing the crossed-key emblem of his office and the bee emblem of his Florentine Barberini family. Leave the square left along Via delle Quattro Fontane past **Palazzo Barberini**, set back in its gardens to retain the air of the family's late-Renaissance country villa built outside what were then the city limits (now a museum including Raphael's *Fornarina*). At the crossroads, **Quadrivio delle Quattro Fontane**, are four allegorical figures of the Tiber and Arno rivers and goddesses Diana and Juno. Turn right on Via del Quirinale. Borromini's **San Carlino** church is a little Baroque masterpiece with convex and concave façade above a statue of St Charles Borromeo. Beyond the first Quirinale gardens, Bernini built the very classical **Sant'Andrea al Quirinale** (1658) while working on St Peter's Square. Stop off in the larger **Giardino del Quirinale** landscaped 1888 for the visit of Kaiser Wilhelm II with a statue of Italy's King Carlo Alberto. The street leads to the solemn **Palazzo del Quirinale**, once a papal summer residence and now the presidential palace.

On the Piazza del Quirinale's **Fontana di Monte Cavallo**, the giant statues of Castor and Pollux reining in their horses were brought here from Augustus's mausoleum. Steps left of the Quirinale palace lead down to Via della Dataria and past the ochre-façaded **Palazzo Testa-Piccolomini**. Continue on Via dell'Umiltà past the churches of Santa Maria dell'Umiltà on the left and Santa Rita on the right to the thriving kosher **Pizzeria da Michele** (No. 31), its unusual fillings popular with Jews and Gentiles alike.

At Piazza dell'Oratorio, the interior of the **Oratorio del Santissimo Crocifisso** is covered with frescoes telling the story of the Cross. Turn right to cross the iron-and-glass-roofed **Galleria Sciarra** shopping arcade (1885). Continue on Santa Maria in Via and turn right on Via delle Muratte. At No. 84, take a peek at the Ristorante Quirino's Art Nouveau décor before ending your walk triumphantly at the **Trevi Fountain**—Euros only. (About 3,000 euros are collected from the fountain every night; the money has been used to subsidize a supermarket for Rome's poor.)

QUIRINAL AND EAST OF CENTRE 51

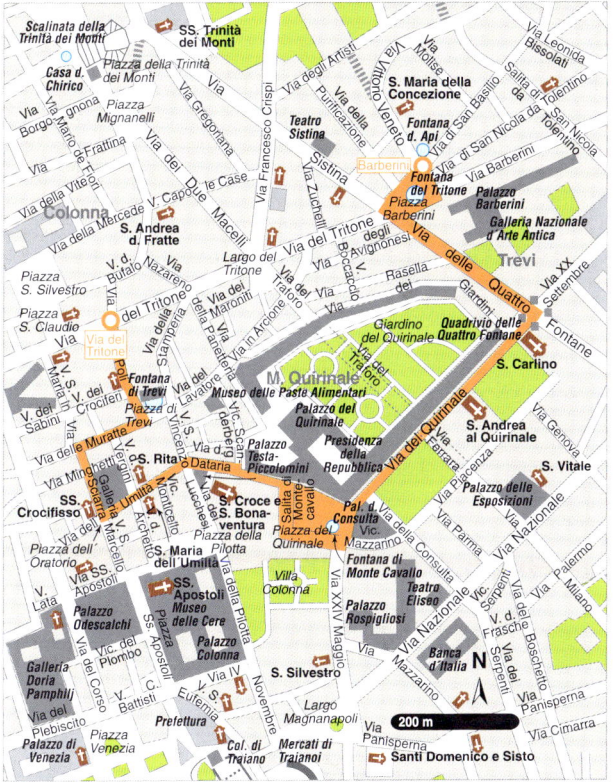

Popes and cardinals had their summer residences here, outside the old city. This walk through gardens and past fountains ends at the most spectacular of all, the Trevi.

Start: Piazza Barberini, Metro Barberini, Bus 62

Finish: Trevi Fountain, Bus 62 (Via del Tritone)

BERNINI'S ROME

Naples-born Gian Lorenzo Bernini (1598–1680) gives the lie to the opinion that nice guys don't make great geniuses. This cheerful, good-hearted fellow learned his craft from his sculptor-father (with whom he designed the Fontana della Barcaccia on Piazza di Spagna) and was equally happy to pass on his knowledge to disciples. The warmth of his character is evident in the exuberance of his sculpture and in the grace and nobility of his architecture.

A 2-hour walk takes in his major works. Departure point is the church of **Santa Maria della Vittoria** (which includes the Cornaro chapel) on Largo Santa Susanna (G2), northwest of Termini railway station. Follow Via Barberini until you reach Piazza Barberini, with its two fountains. Turn into Via delle Quattro Fontane to see the **Palazzo Barberini** (F2). At the next crossroads, walk past the church of San Carlo alle Quattro Fontane (designed by Bernini's rival Borromini) and follow Via del Quirinale (F 3). Admire the long wing of the **Palazzo del Quirinale** and the façade of the exquisite church of **Sant'Andrea al Quirinale**, one of Bernini's greatest achievements.

Take the staircase down to Via della Dataria and Vicolo Scanderbeg, which leads to a little square of the same name, then to Vicolo dei Modelli, where the artists' models used to wait to be hired. You arrive at the Trevi Fountain (E3), which was not designed by Bernini but still reveals the influence he exerted on Roman architectural taste. Leave the square by Via delle Muratte and, at the end of the street, turn right into Via del Corso. You will soon reach Piazza Colonna and then the **Palazzo di Montecitorio**, begun by Bernini and now the seat of the Italian Chamber of Deputies. Via in Aquino leads to the Pantheon. Pope Urban VIII wanted Bernini to redecorate the dome, but the artist refused, declaring that it was perfect as it was. From here, make a small detour to **Piazza della Minerva**, where a little elephant supports a strange obelisk, in front of the church of Santa Maria sopra Minerva. Retrace your steps, then climb the Salita dei Crescenzi to the splendid **Piazza Navona** (D3), redesigned by Bernini for Pope Innocent X. He also designed the **Fontana dei Quattro Fiumi**, but the statues were sculpted by other artists; only the central figure of the **Fontana del Moro** is Bernini's own work. His contemporaries were fascinated by the way he modelled rocks, shells and other natural elements, and by his witty use of water. Push on a little further and you will reach the river banks and the **Ponte Sant'Angelo** (C3), lined with Bernini's windswept angels. To the left, at the end of Via della Conciliazone, is his best-known work, **St Peter's Square** in front of St Peter's Basilica, together with the tombs of the popes, the famous high altar and the bronze *baldacchino* (canopy).

◀ *The Ganges reclines on the Fontana dei Quattro Fiumi.*

▼ *An angel on the Ponte Sant'Angelo.*

TRASTEVERE

In ancient times, foreigners and immigrants settled in this area "across the Tiber", and in the Middle Ages it was the Jewish quarter. A traditional working-class area full of winding alleyways, quaint shops and smart art galleries, it is certainly worth exploring.

THE DISTRICT AT A GLANCE

SIGHTS

Architecture
Fontana dell'Acqua Paola......................55

Art
Galleria Corsini★ 54

Villa Farnesina 54

Churches
Santa Maria in Trastevere 55
Santa Cecilia in Trastevere 55
San Pietro in Montorio 55

Greenery
Parco del Gianicolo★ 55

WALKING TOUR 56

WINING AND DINING 78

Galleria Corsini (Galleria Nazionale d'Arte Antica) (C4) Many distinguished people have stayed in the Corsini Palace—Michelangelo, Bramante, Erasmus and Queen Christina of Sweden, who died here. It contains the large Corsini family collection of 17th- and 18th-century paintings by Lippi, Raphael, Bronzino, Caravaggio, Holbein, Rubens, Van Dyck and more. • **Daily (except Mon) 9am–1.30pm** ☎ 06 6880 2323; guided tours ☎ 06 2258 2493 • Palazzo Corsini, Via della Lungara 10

Villa Farnesina (D4) The wealthy banker Agostino Chigi had this beautiful Renaissance house built by the Siennese architect Baldassare Peruzzi from 1508. Peruzzi also decorated some of the rooms, notably the Sala delle Prospettive, painted in trompe-l'œil to give the illusion of a loggia open to the Roman countryside. Most of the frescoes, however, are the work of Raphael (*The Triumph of Galatea* in the Sala Galatea) or his pupils (*Cupid and Psyche* in the Loggia di Psiche). The villa is surrounded by magnificent gardens. • **Mon–Sat 9am–1pm; mid March–June, mid Sept–Oct and all December 9am–4pm** ☎ 06 6880 1767 • Via della Lungara 230

Santa Maria in Trastevere (D5) This church was probably the first official place of Christian worship built in Rome, dating from the 3rd century. The façade bears a 12th–14th century mosaic of the Virgin and Child with ten maidens. In the apse, mosaics by Pietro Cavallini illustrate six episodes of the life of the Virgin. • Daily 7am–1pm, 4–7pm • Piazza Santa Maria in Trastevere

Santa Cecilia in Trastevere (E5) Saint Cecilia's church is built on the supposed site of her home; she was martyred at the same time as her husband Valerian. The mosaics in the apse were created after 1143. Opposite the altar, a statue by Stefano Maderno (17th century) shows the saint in the position where her body was found, miraculously intact, in the catacombs of San Callisto. Pietro Cavallini's fresco of the *Last Judgement* was discovered in 1900.
• Daily 10am–noon, 4–6pm • Piazza Santa Cecilia

San Pietro in Montorio (C5) A Gothic rose window adorns the façade of this building financed by Ferdinand of Aragon and Isabella of Castille. The two chapels were decorated by pupils of Michelangelo. In the centre of the cloister stands an elegant circular temple *(Tempietto)* by Bramante (1502), located on the supposed site of Saint Peter's crucifixion. • Daily 9am–noon, 4–6pm
• Piazza San Pietro in Montorio 2, Via Garibaldi 33

Fontana dell'Acqua Paola (C5) This fine fountain is shaped like a triumphal arch surmounted by dragons, with monsters in the lateral niches. The three arches give onto a quiet garden. • **Via Garibaldi**

Parco del Gianicolo (C4–5) This large park occupies the top of the Janiculum Hill, offering a splendid panorama of the city. In the middle of the esplanade stands an imposing statue of Garibaldi. There are pony rides and puppet shows, monuments, fountains and a botanical garden.

WALKING TOUR: TRASTEVERE

Get your bearings at the green kiosk tourist office on **Piazza Sidney Sonnino** (prime minister of the early 1900s). East of busy Viale Trastevere, the austere 13th-century **Torre degli Anguillara** now houses a Dante research institute. Across the piazza beyond the Romanesque campanile of **Chiesa San Crisogono** (1124), turn left on Via della Lungaretta to penetrate medieval Trastevere. Flanked by restaurants and ice cream parlours, the parish basilica on **Piazza Santa Maria in Trastevere** was founded by Pope Giulio I (337–352) as Rome's first church open to the public. Opposite is the interesting **Museo di Roma in Trastevere**, with tableaux of wax figures illustrating the history of the district. From the piazza's northeast corner, take Via del Moro, home of a historic pastry shop **Pasticceria Valzani** (No. 37) and **Forno la Renella** (No. 15) reputed to sell the city's best pizza—by the metre. At Piazza Trilussa, a monumental Baroque 17th-century fountain stands across from the popular picnic spot on the **Ponte Sisto** footbridge, originally built by Marcus Aurelius as the city's first link with Trastevere and restored by Pope Sixtus IV.

From the bridge, take the Tiber promenade, **Lungotevere Farnesina**, along the garden side of Baldassare Peruzzi's **Villa Farnesina** (1511) whose Renaissance elegance you can admire by turning left on the narrow Salita del Buon Pastore and left again on Via della Lungara. It stands opposite the long façade of the 18th-century **Palazzo Corsini** (No. 10), now an art museum (Caravaggio's *John the Baptist*, Guido Reni and Annibale Carracci). Continue on Via della Lungara to the castellated **Porta Settimiana** rebuilt in 1498 with the ancient city-wall masonry of Marcus Aurelius. Through the gate on the right is the **John Cabot University** for American students. Double back on Via della Lungara to turn left on Via Corsini down to explore the floral treasures of the **Orto Botanico**, landscaped in 1983 from the palazzo's medieval gardens for the University of Rome's botanical faculty with flora from Sicily's Mount Etna, California, Mexico and Japan.

TRASTEVERE

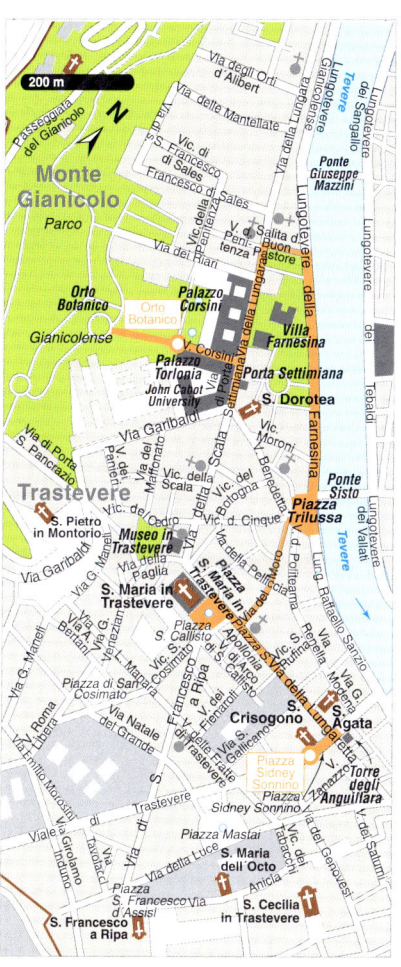

Once the city's Jewish ghetto and working-class district, the gentrified neighbourhood still bears witness to its historical beginnings, with great pizza as a bonus.

Start:
Piazza Sidney Sonnino, Tram 8, Bus H, 23

Finish:
Orto Botanico, Bus 23

VATICAN AREA

A thousand people live and work in the Vatican State. In the 9th century, Pope Leo IV built a wall around the Vatican Hill to protect the basilica built by Constantine over Saint Peter's tomb. This "Leonine" city corresponds to the modern Vatican City. After 1377, the Popes resided in the Apostolic Palaces, which had grown over the centuries to a complex of 1,400 rooms, chambers and chapels. To obtain an audience or take part in ceremonies in the basilica, send a written request to the Prefettura della Casa Pontificia, 00120 Città del Vaticano. Audiences are held every Wednesday (when the Pope is in Rome), generally at 11 a.m.

THE DISTRICT AT A GLANCE

SIGHTS

Architecture
Castel Sant'Angelo ★ 58
Piazza San Pietro ★ ..59

Church
San Pietro in Vaticano 60

Museums
Musei Vaticani 60
Cappella Sistina ★ 61

Necropoli dell'Autoparco 63

WALKING TOUR 64

WINING AND DINING 79

Castel Sant'Angelo (C2) Built in AD 139 as a mausoleum for the Emperor Hadrian, this fortress became successively an outpost of the Aurelian Wall, a citadel, a medieval prison and a residence of the Popes (who linked it to the Vatican by building the *passetto*, a passage in the walls). It was named Sant'Angelo by Pope Gregory the Great who, while riding in a procession during an epidemic of plague, had a vision of the Archangel Saint Michael replacing his sword in its sheath. This was interpreted as a sign that the plague was coming to an end. The Castel is now home to the National Museum: exploring its 58 rooms you retrace the entire history of the building, which also houses collections of ceramics, ancient weapons, paintings and decorative items. Ponte Sant'Angelo, the bridge which spans the Tiber in front of the Castel, is one of the most handsome in the city. The ten baroque angels in white marble, their robes blowing in the wind, were designed by Gian Lorenzo Bernini and sculpted

From the terrace of St Peter's dome, you get a splendid view of the Eternal City.

by Roman artists under his guidance. Each one bears an instrument of Christ's martyrdom. *The Recording Angel* was sculpted largely by Bernini himself: his two other angels, judged by the Pope as too precious to be exposed to the elements, were placed in the church of Sant'Andrea delle Fratte. • Daily (except Mon) 9am–8pm, sometimes later in summer • Lungotevere Castello 50

Piazza San Pietro (B2–3) From Sant'Angelo, the Via della Conciliazione leads directly to this magnificent square, built between 1656 and 1667 by Bernini. Oval in shape, the square is 240 m (787 ft) wide and 196 m (643 ft) long, watched over by 140 stone saints and surrounded by four rows of columns (284 in all). To see the columns dissolve into a single row, stand on one of the two discs set in the ground half-way between the obelisk and the fountains. The obelisk was brought from Alexandria to ornament the ancient Circus of Caligula which stood to the left of the present basilica. It was moved to the centre of St Peter's Square in 1586, an operation which took four months and required the efforts of 900 men, 47 cranes and 150 horses. The cross on the top is believed to contain a fragment of the True Cross.

San Pietro in Vaticano (B3) Saint Peter was put to death in the Circus of Caligula in the year 64. In the 2nd century, a sanctuary was erected around his tomb in the necropolis north of the Circus. Constantine built a great basilica on the same site, which was completed in about 349. It was falling into ruin by 1506 when Pope Julius II laid the foundation stone of a new building. This took more than a century to complete, with all the great Renaissance and baroque artists contributing to the work. The vastness of the basilica is difficult to comprehend: it measures 187 m (613 ft) in length and contains 11 chapels, 45 altars and countless works of art. Bronze markers in the floor show the dimensions of other great churches, all inferior to St Peter's, of course. The two lateral naves, 76 m (249 ft) long, end under the enormous dome by Michelangelo. One of the same artist's most beautiful works, the marble sculpture of the Pietà, which he completed before the age of 25, is in a chapel near the entrance, protected by a glass screen. Bernini's extravagant bronze *baldacchino* above the high altar is as tall as the Palazzo Farnese. You can take the lift to the Loggia degli Apostoli and then climb the steps to enjoy the view from the terrace. There is access from the basilica to the papal tombs, St Peter's tomb and the Scavi (excavations), a necropolis discovered in the 1940s. A well-preserved street is lined with brick mausolea and family tombs. • **Basilica daily 7am– 6pm; Sun 8am– 4.45pm** • **For 75-min tours of the Scavi, book in advance, specifying date, names, number of participants and language to the Ufficio degli Scavi, fax 06 6987 3017 or e-mail uff.scavi@fsp.va** • **Piazza San Pietro**

Musei Vaticani (B2) The Renaissance palaces built by Popes Sixtus IV, Innocent VII and Julius II house one of the most important art collections in the world. The courtyards and galleries were designed by Bramante in 1503. The later extensions date from the 18th century, when for the first time the priceless works of art were put on public view. You have to follow one of the four colour-coded routes, all of which pass through the Sistine Chapel. The shortest lasts 90 minutes, the longest takes a strenuous 5 hours. Concentrate on one collection and to plan for short breaks to give your feet—and your brain—a rest. Below we describe the Sistine Chapel and a selection of the most interesting museums.

• Mon–Fri and last Sun of month (free entrance) from 10am; closing time varies from 12.30 to 3.30pm depending on the season. Sat 10am–12.30pm. Closed on national and religious holidays. • For the Necropoli dell'Autoparco, open for visitors Fri and Sat, book in advance to Ufficio Visite Speciali, e-mail to visitedidattiche.musei@scv.va • Entrance on the Viale Vaticano to the right of St Peter's Square. • www.vatican.va

Cappella Sistina (B2) Famous the world over, the Sistine Chapel owes its name to the pope who first had it built, Sixtus IV. (It is the room the cardinals use when they meet to elect a new pope.) From 1475 onwards, with a vast fund of church money at his disposal, Sixtus commissioned the greatest artists of the time—Pinturicchio, Perugino, Botticelli, Ghirlandaio, Signorelli, Rosselli—to cover the walls with frescoes illustrating the lives of Moses and Jesus Christ. On Michelangelo's ceiling, more than 300 figures illustrate the creation of mankind. In the centre is the scene of Eve's creation, and just next to it, the best-known image, where God stretches out a finger to create Adam. It was Pope Julius II who persuaded the sculptor to take on this task. Unfamiliar with fresco techniques, Michelangelo was reluctant to accept the challenge posed by the ceiling's enormous dimensions and its vaulted shape. The resulting masterpiece was to prove that he was on a par with the greatest artists of his time. He soon fired his assistants as incompetent, and spent four uncomfortable years, from 1508 to 1512, completing the majestic fresco, standing precariously on tiptoe on a mobile scaffolding he designed himself, his head craned backwards. Julius II, anxious to

SWISS GUARD

Cohors Pedestris Helvetiorum a Sacra Custodia Pontificis is the Vatican's name for the Swiss Guard. Sixtus IV hired this troop of Swiss infantrymen in 1480 and his nephew Julius II gave them their formal status in 1506. They proved their valour and sense of self-sacrifice on May 6, 1527, when 147 Guards died fighting the troops of Charles V during the Sack of Rome while 40 survivors escorted Clement VII to safety. Ever since, May 6 is official swearing-in day for recruits, who must be at least 1.74 m tall and aged between 19 and 30.

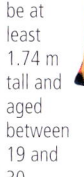

see the work completed, hassled him constantly, threatening to topple him down from the scaffolding if he didn't hurry up. Twenty-three years later, at the age of 60, Michelangelo began work on the *Last Judgement*, covering the wall behind the high altar. It took him another seven years to finish the cataclysmic scene, the action swirling round a stern-faced Christ dispensing justice. The nudity of the figures offended Pope Paul IV who had some of them painted over with wispy veils by Daniele da Volterra. This earned him the nickname il Braghettone, "the pants-maker". Michelangelo incorporated a deformed self-portrait into the painting: look at the flayed skin held by Saint Bartholomew just below Christ. Restoration of the Sistine Chapel was begun almost by accident in 1979. During a routine clean-up of the frescoes, someone scratched a corner of the ceiling and noticed the brilliant colours hidden beneath a thick layer of dust and greasy soot from centuries of candles. A detailed inspection revealed that cracks had been caused by the application of glues in preceding restorations. Financed by the Japanese television company NTV, which was granted the rights to film the entire venture, the restoration took the Vatican's team 13 years to complete. A special mixture of fungicide, ammonium bicarbonate and sodium bicarbonate was applied to dissolve the impurities, which were then carefully wiped off with a sterilized natural sponge. The result was controversial, as most people were taken aback at the vibrance of colours and the clear outlines of the figures. Sit on a bench near the chapel exit to best judge it for yourself.

Appartamenti Borgia The Borgia Appartments are decorated with frescoes by Pinturicchio, portraits of famous Borgias, bronzes by Rodin, ceramics by Picasso, and more.

Biblioteca Apostolica The frescoed halls of the Vatican Library contain 1.8 million rare books and ancient manuscripts, including a 4th-century Gospel of Saint Matthew and a text by Luther. (Closed for renovation till 2010)

Cappella del Beato Angelico In the Chapel of Nicolas V, luminous frescoes by Fra Angelico illustrate the lives of Saint Stephen and Saint Laurence.

Collezione d'Arte Religiosa Moderna Modern religious art: works by Dali, Kandinski, Klee, Matisse, Modigliani, Picasso, Utrillo and more.

Museo Chiaramonti Greek and Roman statuary.

Museo Filatelico e Numismatico Beautiful postage stamps and coins issued by the Vatican State.

Museo Gregoriano Egizio Egyptian pieces from temples and gardens in and around Rome, including copies from Hadrian's villa at Tivoli.

Museo Gregoriano Etrusco Etruscan sarcophagi, statues, bronzes, pottery, glassware and jewellery from the 7th century BC.

Museo Gregoriano Profano Greek and Roman antiquities.

Museo Missionario-Etnologico Accounts by Catholic missionaries, of social and cultural interest.

Museo Pio-Clementino Greek and Roman sculpture reclaimed at the time of the demolition of ancient monuments in the 16th century, notably the Laocoon group, dug up in a vineyard on the Esquiline Hill in 1506.

Museo Pio Cristiano Pieces excavated from the catacombs depicting the lives of the early Christians.

Museo Storico Vaticano The history of the Vatican and the Papal States, with a collection of antique "popemobiles" (in San Giovanni in Laterano, H6).

Necropoli dell'Autoparco Discovered in 2003 during construction of a multi-storey carpark, this necropolis was set along the Via Triumphalis; 40 burial structures and more than 200 tombs were found, in an excellent state of preservation, as well as urns, sculpted sarcophagi, altars, mosaic floors. The finds date from the end of the 1st century BC to the beginning of the 4th century.

Pinacoteca The Art Gallery consists of fifteen rooms and ten centuries of unforgettable paintings: Caravaggio, Domenichino, Giotto, Fra Angelico, Perugino, Leonardo Da Vinci.

Stanze di Raffaello Four rooms decorated for Pope Julius II by the artist as a young man. Of particular note is the Stanza della Segnatura (Signature Room).

WALKING TOUR: AROUND THE VATICAN

From the riverside Piazza della Rovere, a narrow street leads to the ancient Roman city-walls and **Porta Santo Spirito**, Antonio da Sangallo's monumental gateway interrupted in 1543 because it conflicted with Michelangelo's design for the Vatican's fortifications. Beyond the gate, Via dei Penitenzieri passes a Baroque archway of the German pilgrims' **Ospedale di Santo Spirito in Sassia** (No. 13) and its church at the corner. Turn right past the governor of the Santo Spirito Fraternity's 16th-century **Palazzo del Commendatore** and the 15th-century colonnaded **Corsia Sistina**. At the east end of the triangular complex is a medical museum, **Museo dell'Arte Sanitaria**, whose collections include surgical instruments from ancient Rome and Arabia. Across from the corner of Borgo Santo Spirito and Lungotevere Vaticano, the fraternity's 18th-century church **Santa Maria Annunziata** was transported here during the construction of Via della Conciliazione.

Walk left along the river to the grandiose **Castel Sant'Angelo** at the end of its monumental bridge and the beginning of **Via della Conciliazione**. To make place for this processional route and clear the view of St Peter's, other churches were moved, palazzi rebuilt and the medieval neighbourhood between Borgo Santo Spirito and Borgo Sant'Angelo was razed, all in time for the Holy Year in 1950. On the right is the stiff and sober travertine and white limestone **Santa Maria in Traspontina** (1587). On the same side, at No. 30, is the Renaissance **Palazzo Torlonia**, built for Henry VIII's English ambassador to the Vatican. Opposite is the Tuscan-style 15th-century **Palazzo dei Penitenzieri**, now a hotel but originally built for Cardinal Domenico della Rovere and used by father confessors for wealthy penitents under Pope Alexander VII.

As you continue towards Bernini's **Piazza San Pietro**, notice the symmetrical obelisk lampposts expressly designed to compensate for the irregularities of the street's façades and achieve the desired spiritual harmony for the pilgrims.

THE VATICAN 65

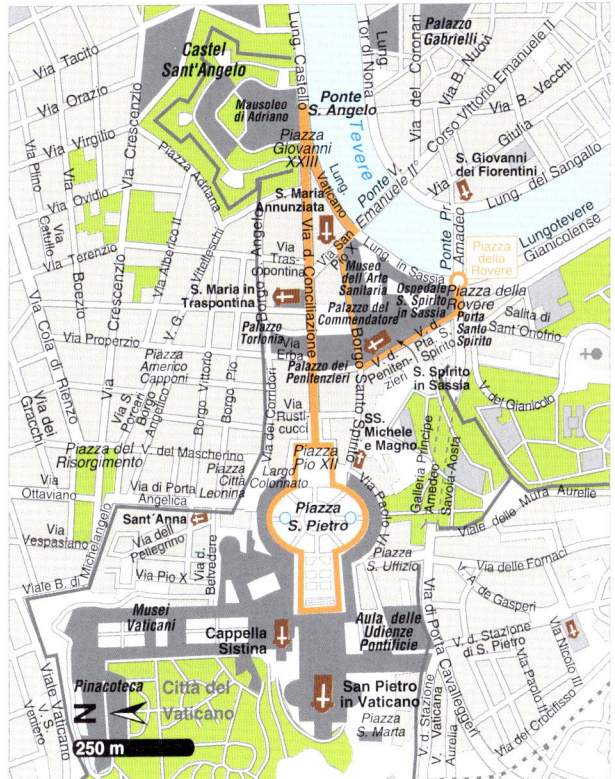

Visit what is left of the old Santo Spirito neighbourhood left by medieval German pilgrims before taking the grand procession route to St Peter's.

Start and finish:
Piazza della Rovere, Bus 23 (Lungotevere in Sassia)

EXCURSIONS

When you can't face another painting and you're suffering from an overload of golden cherubs, take the metro or a train and get out of the city centre.

EXCURSIONS AT A GLANCE

SIGHTS

Ancient sites
Ostia Antica............69

Architecture
EUR 68

Art
Art Center Acea 67

Atmosphere
Cimitero Acattolico ..66
Testaccio 66
Castelli Romani 68
Fregene 68
Civitavecchia 69

Greenery
Tivoli ★ 69

Church
San Paolo fuori
le Mura 67

Museums
EUR 68
Villa Adriana............69

WINING AND DINING 79

Cimitero Acattolico (off map, dir. E6) Spread out at the foot of the marble-faced Cestius Pyramid (the mausoleum of praetor Caius Cestus), this cemetery (also called Cimitero Protestante) is one of the most romantic places in Rome. Beneath the dark shade of pines and cypresses, in the company of many other "non-Catholics"—Protestants, Orthodox, Jews, atheists and anyone else not admitted to the Catholic cemeteries (except actors and anyone having committed suicide), lie the English poets Keats and Shelley, Goethe's only son, and Antonio Gramsci, founder of the Italian communist party. • Mon–Sat (except holidays) 9am–5pm (last entrance 4.30pm). • Via Caio Cestio 6 Ⓜ B to Piramide

Testaccio (off map, dir. E 6) In ancient times, cargoes of wine, oil and wheat were delivered to Rome in clay amphoras, which were emptied, smashed up and the shards thrown onto a dump. The dump grew into a 35-m-high hill, Monte Testaccio, where the Romans built a marble warehouse. At the end of the 19th century the Testaccio became a working-class neighbourhood, clustered around a slaughterhouse. It has now developed into an entertainment centre,

At close quarters in Rocca di Papa, a small town of the Alban Hills.

with friendly restaurants and a lively nightlife. Bars and discotheques have been gouged out of the side of the hill, and you can still make out the odd fragment of amphora embedded in the walls. • **Between via Marmorata and the river** Ⓜ B to Piramide

Art Center Acea (off map, dir. E 6) "Machines and Gods", a fascinating exhibition of 400 marble statues from the Capitoline museums, placed in the unlikely setting of a disused power station. • **Tues–Fri, Sun 9.30am–7pm; Sat 9.30am–6pm** ☎ 06 57 991 • **Centrale Montemartini, Via Ostiense 106** Ⓜ B to Piramide or Garbatella

San Paolo fuori le Mura (off map, dir. E 6) The Church of St Paul's Outside the Walls is a faithful reconstruction of the great 4th century basilica devastated by fire in 1823. There is a splendid Venetian mosaic (1220) in the apse. A tomb believed to be that of Saint Paul was excavated from beneath the altar in 2006

and is awaiting authentification. The cloister, built in 1208 and spared by the flames, is one of the finest in Rome. In the centre is a charming rose garden.
• Daily 7am–7pm • Via Ostiense 186   Ⓜ B to Basilica San Paolo

EUR, Esposizione Universale di Roma (map 3) Begun on the orders of Mussolini, for a Universal Exposition that never took place because of World War II, this district of glassy office blocks and stark apartment buildings, 5 km (3 miles) south of Rome, has some interesting examples of monumental Fascist architecture and several museums. The Museo della Civiltà Romana on piazza G. Agnelli traces the history of Rome. Its highlight is a scale model of the imperial city, depicting every building inside the Aurelian Wall. The Museo Nazionale Preistorico ed Etnografico Luigi Pigorini, on the corner of Piazza Marconi and viale Lincoln, studies the people of the world, and there's a collection of local prehistoric finds. The Museo Nazionale delle Arti e Tradizioni Popolari on the other side of Piazza Marconi illustrates Italian customs and traditions, displaying household utensils and agricultural tools, pottery, jewellery and other objects. • Museo della Civiltà Romana: daily (except Mon) 9am–2pm ☎ 06 592 6135 • Museo Pigorini: daily (except Mon) 9am–8pm ☎ 06 549 521 • Museo delle Arti e Tradizioni Popolari: Tues–Fri 9am–6pm, Sat–Sun and holidays 9am–8pm ☎ 06 591 0709   Ⓜ B to Fermi

Castelli Romani In the Middle Ages, several castles were built in the foothills of the Colli Albani 12 km (7 miles) southeast of Rome: these became fortified villages and then developed into small hill towns. This is where modern Romans spend their weekends. You will be spoilt for choice: Frascati and its splendid villas, in particular Villa Aldobrandini; Castel Gandolfo, the summer residence of the Pope; Ariccia with its baroque palaces by Bernini; Genzano, famous for the Corpus Domini festival in May or June when a carpet of flowers covers the steps up to the church of Santa Maria della Cima; Rocca di Papa; Monte Compatri; and many others. • Ⓜ A to Anagnina then bus (trips from 30 –90 min).

Fregene An elegant beach resort, 38 km (24 miles) from Rome. Pope Clement IX, one of the landowners, planted a pine forest along the shore as protection from the Mediterranean winds. Today it makes a superb backdrop for the villas and golden sands. • Ⓜ A to Lepanto, then CoTral bus to Fregene (1hr)

EXCURSIONS 69

Ostia Antica In ancient times, Ostia, 25 km (16 miles) southwest of Rome, was the city's thriving main commercial port, directly on the coast. Then it silted up and was abandoned because of malaria; it lay buried under sand for centuries. West of the site entrance, the main street, Decumanus Maximus, leads past the Neptune Baths to Piazzale delle Corporazioni, Ostia's main square, where mosaics in front of the shops and offices indicate the owner's trade—nautical gear, grain merchants, rope-makers. Bordering the square, the theatre was expanded in the 2nd century to take 4,000 spectators. Left of the square beyond the *horrea* (warehouses), the Casa di Diana is the town's best-preserved residence, built around a square atrium with a family shrine to the cult of Mithras and rooftop view over the site. North of this house, the museum displays sculpture, murals and mosaics. • **Daily (except Mon) 8.30am–4pm (Jan, Feb, Nov, Dec), 5pm (Mar), 6pm (Apr–Oct)** Ⓜ B to Magliana, then train to Ostia Antica (about 20 min)

Tivoli Just 30 km (19 miles) from Rome, this is where the ancient Romans used to spend their holidays. You can stroll in the gardens of splendid villas: Villa d'Este with its grottoes and fountains; Villa Gregoriana and its tree-filled garden; and Villa Adriana (Hadrian's Villa), a vast open-air museum illustrating all the ostentation of the Roman Empire. • **Villa Adriana daily 9am–1 hour before sunset** ☎ 07 7453 0203 Ⓜ B to Ponte Mammolo then CoTral bus to Tivoli, or train FS line FM2 to Tivoli and bus CAT4

Civitavecchia The town, 80 km (50 miles) northwest of Rome, has been rebuilt since its large-scale destruction in World War II. On the harbour, it has preserved the 16th-century Fort Michelangelo, commissioned by Pope Julius II and begun by Bramante and Sangallo before the keep was completed by Michelangelo. The remains of a Roman villa have been excavated within its precincts. North of the modern harbour, the ancient Roman port (Darsena romana) originally laid out by Emperor Trajan now provides mooring for the fishing fleet. The city walls here date back to the Renaissance. Remains of the *centro storico* are behind Corso Marconi, including the Duomo. One of the town's more interesting churches is the 19th-century Chiesa dei Santissimi Martiri Giapponesi (Holy Japanese Martyrs) dedicated to 26 Franciscans crucified at Nagasaki in 1597.
• **Train FS from Roma Termini (about 1 hr 20 min)**

CHILDREN'S ROME

In a country where people are so in love with their kids, it comes as a surprise that the city of Rome has so few sightseeing attractions to offer specifically for children. Not that there's nothing at all, but it takes a little planning to keep them happy.

Eating out

Luckily, sightseeing is not everything, and the Italians are champions in the thing that is really important to children—food. No kids should ever be sad in a town with the world's greatest ice cream and pretty terrific pasta and pizza. In fact, pizza is the one food that you can be sure of finding all day long, to save waiting for the 8pm opening times for most "grown-up" restaurants. Even the smartest of the latter do not present a practical problem—this when the Italians' love of kids kicks in. For the very small, a high chair *(seggiolone)* is almost always available, and for those who don't like pasta with sauces too spicy or otherwise "weird", ask for tomato-sauce *pasta al pomodoro* or plain *pasta in bianco* with just oil or butter and parmesan. But they—and you—may be surprised how quickly they take to the "weird" stuff, too, like seafood (even octopus!) if they try some of yours.

Two Parks and a Fairground

The best of the public parks and gardens is the **Villa Borghese**—entrance off Piazzale Flaminio with its playground, pedalos on its artificial lake, little zoo, pony-drawn train and bicycles for hire. The **Parco del Gianicolo** south of the Vatican is popular for its old-fashioned puppet shows and pony rides.

Luna Park (also known as Luna EUR) is an old-fashioned amusement park—Ferris wheel, swings and roundabouts—just outside Rome at Via delle Tre Fontane (metro B line to EUR Fermi station).

Museums

Yes, there are museums that kids can enjoy. The best is **Explora**, Via Flaminia 82, for children under 12. Housed in a converted tram depot from the 1870s, it is not at all commercial but a highly entertaining and educational hands-on exploration of the worlds of communications, technology and the environment. It provides an astonishing primer both in Newtonian physics and how to anchor a TV news show. Visits last 1 hr 45 min. Daily (except Mon) at 10am (except in August), noon, 3 and 5 pm. ☎ 06 361 3776

More spooky is the **Museo Criminologico di Roma**, Via del Gonfalone 29. This former prison traces the grim history of Italy's prison system, showing how the police solve crimes and, best of all for the kids, the gory punishments inflicted over the centuries. Tues–Sat 9am–1pm; Tues, Thurs also 2.30–6.30pm. ☎ 06 6830 0234

The Crypt to End All Crypts

While we're doing spooky, visit the crypt of the 17th-century **Chiesa della Immacolata Concezione**, Via Vittorio Veneto 27, less *dolce vita* than *dolce morte*. In the crypt, the Capuchin Friars *(Frati Cappuccini)* designed the most gloriously gruesome monuments to their departed brethren. Using skulls, shoulder blades, pelvis-bones, tibia and thigh-bones, they have fashioned an hour-glass, floral motifs, canopies, rosettes, eight-pointed stars and a Crucifixion with a crown composed of minute vertebrae. Kids love it. Daily (except Thurs) 9am–noon, 3–6pm.

On a More Cheerful Note

The one ancient Roman monument that children do seem to enjoy is the **Colosseum**, though even there, some of them will want to know how many Christians were fed to the lions (sorry, no-one kept a tally). They also love putting their hands in the **Bocca della Verità** (see p. 21).

cityBites

In the restaurants and trattorie listed here you can eat well at a fairly reasonable price. If you're just looking for a snack, try an *enoteca*, or wine bar, which serves local specialities as well as wine. Bars and cafés also sell delicious sandwiches, hot toasted *panini* and irresistible pastries. There's nowhere better for a short rest and the chance to observe Rome's *dolce vita*.

   A typical Roman menu might begin with *bruschette* (toast rubbed with garlic and oil). Then comes the pasta: *bucatini alla matriciana* or *spaghetti alla carbonara*. Next, the main course of meat, often served with vegetables: *coda alla vaccinara* (oxtail), *abbacchio al forno* (roast lamb), *scottadito* (lamb chop), *saltimbocca alla romana* (thin slices of veal with ham and sage). Don't miss the *carciofi* (artichokes), prepared *alla romana* or *alla giudia*. Room for dessert? Home-made ice cream, of course! As for wines, the best-known Roman white is Frascati, but Castelli Romani, Marino, Colli Albani, Velletri and Verdicchio are also very drinkable. The reds are mostly from other areas of Italy.

1 up to €20   2 up to €50   3 over €50

ANCIENT ROME

Apuleius
Via Tempio di Diana 15
☎ 06 574 2160
Closed Sat lunch, Sun
[3]
Part of an ancient Roman wall is incorporated into the dining room of this elegant restaurant in the Aventino district. Refined cuisine, unusually spiced and beautifully served.

HISTORIC CENTRE

Achilli al Parlamento
Via dei Prefetti 15
☎ 06 687 3446
Closed Sun
[1]
A wine bar, *enoteca*, where you can choose from a variety of open sandwiches, cold buffet, pies and pastries along with a glass of good Italian wine such as Barolo or Sassicaia.

Ad Hoc
Via di Ripetta 43
☎ 06 323 3040
[2]
The building dates from 1500 and the original ceiling is still visible. Popular with businessmen, noted for its fish menu, and renowned for the fresh pasta with truffles and clams. Good wine list.

AL 34
Via Mario de' Fiori 34
☎ 06 679 5091
Closed Mon
[2]
Excellent food, enjoyable atmosphere. Try the ravioli with 34 herbs!

Al Pompiere
Via Santa Maria dei Calderari 38
☎ 06 686 8377
Closed Sun
[2]
On the first floor of the Cenci Palace, in the heart of the Jewish Ghetto, this restaurant serves typical local cuisine beneath a lovely wood-beam ceiling; the menu includes ancient Roman dishes. Great value for money.

Antica Enoteca
Via della Croce 76B
☎ 06 679 0896
Closed mid August
[1]
A delightfully old-fashioned wine bar and restaurant with good, down-to-earth Roman cooking; one of the city's best secrets. It also sells olive oil and *grappa*.

Antica Enoteca Beccaria
Via C. Beccaria 14
☎ 06 321 7357
Closed Sat afternoon
[1]
Off Piazzale Flaminio, a few tables and a bar for sampling Italian wine, cheese, salami and roast pork *(porchetto)*.

Antico Caffè Greco
Via Condotti 86
☎ 06 679 1700
Liszt, Gogol, Goethe and many other celebrities have frequented this attractive old café which was founded in 1760.

Antico Caffè della Pace
Via della Pace 3–7
☎ 06 686 1216
[2]
Traditional café north of Piazza Navona very popular with writers and artists. Delicious chocolate desserts.

Babington's Tea Rooms
Piazza di Spagna 23
☎ 06 678 6027
Closed Tues
Founded by two English ladies in 1893, this establishment with the trademark black cat still serves real English tea (and many other fine blends), scones, jams and crumpets.

Bar del Fico
Piazza del Fico 26/28
☎ 06 686 5205
Closed Sun morning
Frequented by actors, artists and politicians who

put the world to rights under the superb fig tree.

Bevitoria Navona
Piazza Navona 72
☎ 06 6880 1022
1
Italian wines, snacks and other appetizers.

Caffè Farnese
Via dei Baullari 106
☎ 06 6880 2125
Well located near the Piazza Farnese, with plenty of outside tables for watching the world go by. A great meeting place.

Ciampini al Café du Jardin
Piazza Trinità dei Monti 1
☎ 06 678 5678
Closed Wed (except in summer)
2
The perfect place to sip your apéritif or enjoy an ice cream as you watch the sun set over the Eternal City. Roof garden and restaurant.

Corallo
Via del Corallo 10
☎ 06 6830 7703
Daily noon–4 p.m. and 7 p.m.–1 a.m.
1
A good choice of pizzas with thin crispy crust, as well as *focacce*. Tues and Fri main dishes based on fish and mixed grills.

Cul de Sac
Piazza Pasquino 73
☎ 06 6880 1094
1
Tiny wine bar with two rows of tables. Italian cheeses and smoked meats, bean soup, Greek salad, desserts. Very popular, no bookings.

Da Baffetto
Via del Governo Vecchio 11
☎ 06 686 1617
7pm–midnight
1
A Roman institution, famed for its enormous pizzas; you may have to queue and share a table.

Ditirambo
Piazza della Cancelleria 74/75
☎ 06 687 1626
Closed Mon lunch
Best to book
2
Small and lively trattoria with a slightly chaotic atmosphere. Excellent fresh pasta, vegetarian dishes, divine desserts.

Gelateria della Palma
Via della Maddalena 20/23
☎ 06 6880 6752
Exquisite ices. It's absolutely agonizing to have to choose, with more than 100 flavours on offer. How about dark chocolate with candied orange peel?

Giolitti
Via degli Uffici del Vicario 40
☎ 06 699 1243
Sample incredible ice cream creations in this famous gelateria near Piazza di Montecitorio: a Torre Eiffel, almost as big as the real Eiffel Tower, or the fantastic Coppa Olimpica Mondiale.

Il Gusto
Piazza Augusto Imperatore 9,
Via della Frezza 23
☎ 06 322 6273
2
A classy restaurant in black, white and wicker, featuring "creative Mediterranean cuisine", with a menu changing every four months. There is also a pizzeria, a wine bar, a bookshop library devoted to wine, and a shop selling all sorts of gourmet gifts, regional products and designer kitchen utensils. Just north of Mausoleo di Augusto.

Il Valentino
Via della Fontanella 14
☎ 06 361 0880
Open April to October
3
The refined restaurant of the Hotel Valadier, with

roof garden, between Via del Babuino and Via del Corso. Creative, seasonal Italian cuisine.

La Campana
Vicolo della Campana 18/20
☎ 06 687 5273
Closed Mon
[2]

Set in a 16th-century palace near Montecitorio, it claims to be the oldest restaurant in Rome. Delicious artichokes fried in olive oil, tasty *tagliolini* with anchovies and pecorino cheese.

La Penna d'Oca
Via della Penna 53
☎ 06 320 2898
Evenings only; closed Sun
[2]

Mostly fish and seafood prepared in unusual ways, but the menu includes meat dishes, too. Home-made desserts such as hot pear tart.

La Rosetta
Via della Rosetta 8
☎ 06 686 1002
Closed Sat, Sun lunch
Reservation recommended
[3]

Rome's first and finest fish-only restaurant founded in 1966 and now run by the son of the original owners. Right on the doorstep of the Pantheon.

La Taverna di Giovanni
Via del Banco di Santo Spirito 58
☎ 06 686 4116
Closed Mon
[1]

Opposite Castel Sant' Angelo, simple and basic Roman specialities: *rigatoni alla matriciana*, gnocchi, tripe, at very reasonable prices.

La Vecchia Bottega
Via S. Maria del Pianto 9A/11
☎ 06 6819 2210
Closed Sun and Mon
[1]

Wine bar run by brothers, Gino and Antonio, serving cold meals made from ultra-fresh ingredients—salads, carpaccios and *involtini* (rolls with various stuffings). Near Campo dei Fiori.

Margutta Vegetariano
Via Margutta 111
☎ 06 3265 0577
[2]

Vegetarians, vegans, look no further. Inspired and tasty dishes, mostly organic, on a quiet but beautiful street full of artists' studios. They even manage to make tofu exciting.

Myosotis
Vicolo della Vaccarella 3/5
☎ 06 686 5554
Closed Sun, Mon lunch
[2]

Delicious *frittura mista* (mixed fried fish), grilled buffalo steak, baked swordfish stuffed with cheese, freshly baked bread—like the forget-me-not of its name, memorable!

Osteria del Sostegno
Via delle Colonnelle 5
☎ 06 679 3842
Closed Mon
[1]

An attractive place in an alley behind the Pantheon with an extensive and varied menu.

Osteria dell'Antiquario
Piazzetta S. Simeone 26
☎ 06 687 9694
Closed Sun
[2] – [3]

In medieval stone stables, a chic restaurant serving traditional dishes adapted to modern tastes.

Otello alla Concordia
Via della Croce 81
☎ 06 679 1178
Closed Sun
Book ahead
[2]

A restaurant specializing in fish, in the courtyard of an 18th-century palace.

Pancrazio
Piazza del Biscione 92
☎ 06 686 1246
Closed Wed
[2]
Built in the ruins of Pompey's theatre. Excellent seafood risotto.

Porto di Ripetta
Via di Ripetta 250
☎ 06 361 2376
Closed Sun
[2]
You dine in the basement beneath ancient brick vaults. Fish dishes only, imaginatively prepared.

La Sagrestia
Via del Seminario 89
☎ 06 679 7581
Closed Wed
[1]
Classic Roman, Tuscan and Mediterranean cuisine.

Sant'Eustachio
Piazza Sant'Eustachio 82
☎ 06 654 2048
Near the Pantheon, one of the most famous cafés in Rome, serving its best coffee, *gran caffè*.

Settimio all'Arancio
Via dell'Arancio 50
☎ 06 687 6119
Closed Sun
[2]
In a décor of Etruscan inspiration, inventive meat and fish dishes.

Vecchia Roma
Piazza Campitelli 12
☎ 06 686 4604
Closed Wed
[1]
A church converted to a restaurant, north of Teatro di Marcello. Salads in summer, polenta with meat, fish and vegetables in winter, as well as pasta and risottos.

QUIRINAL AND EAST OF CENTRE

Al Boschetto
Via del Boschetto 30
☎ 06 474 4770
Closed Sun lunch
[1]
Fresh and wholesome food; the main speciality is mushrooms.

Al Ceppo
Via Panama 2
☎ 06 855 1379
Closed Mon
[2]
Meat grilled on an open fireplace (try the beef fillet with black truffles) and fabulous desserts. Stop by on your way to the Catacombs of Priscilla.

Al Moro
Vicolo delle Bollette 13
☎ 06 678 3495
Closed Sun
[2]
An authentic trattoria, a great place for *abbacchio*

A BRIEF HISTORY OF ICE CREAM

Among the many good things Marco Polo is credited with bringing back from China in the 13th century, let us give thanks for ice cream. Actually, he was not the first Italian to dabble in this cold ambrosia. Nero used to serve a delicious concoction of puréed fruits, honey and snow. The undisputed masters of Italian *gelati* at the end of the 18th century were Signori Pratti and Tortoni, who toured the courts of Europe with their frozen delicacies. Then, in the early 20th century, the US laid claim to world supremacy—not long after the first wave of Italians had passed through immigration.

(tender milk-fed lamb with rosemary).

Alfredo a Via Gabi
Via Gabi 36
☎ 06 7720 6792
Closed Tues
[2]
A large trattoria with a pergola behind San Giovanni in Laterano. Rich

food, copiously served: try pasta with mushrooms in cream sauce or *straccetti al gorgonzola*: finely sliced beef in a cheese sauce.

Arancia blu
Via dei Latini 55/65
☎ 06 445 4105
Open every evening from 8.30 p.m.
Reservation advised.
[2]
A trendy, arty restaurant for gourmet vegetarians and wine connoisseurs.

Café de Paris
Via Vittorio Veneto 90
☎ 06 481 5631
[2]
The meeting place for the dolce vita crowd, with restaurant, bar, pasticceria and gelateria.

Cantina Cantarini
Piazza Sallustio 12
☎ 06 485 528
Closed Sun
[2]
Exellent *fritto misto*, and a wide choice of pasta with fish or meat sauces. From Thurs evening to Sat, fish from the Adriatic. Friendly atmosphere, near Porta Pia.

Cesarina
Via Piemonte 109
☎ 06 4201 3432
Closed Sun
[2]
Specialities from Rome and also from the Emilia-Romagna district in Northern Italy, with good fish dishes.

Da Franco ar Vicoletto
Via dei Falisci 1A/2
☎ 06 495 7675
Closed Mon
Reservation advised
[1]
The freshest of fish prepared in many original and delectable ways.

Da Robertino
Via Panisperna 231
☎ 06 474 0620
Closed Mon
[2]
Classic yet inventive cuisine in this elegant restaurant. Champagne risotto, fish and good meat dishes, exquisitely served by a friendly staff.

Est! Est!! Est!!!
Via Genova 32
☎ 06 488 1107
Closed Mon
[1]
This is one of Rome's best-known pizzerias, on the street running between the Via Nazionale and the Ministry of the Interior. Drink in the boisterous atmosphere while you enjoy a *calzone* (folded pizza) or the *filetti di baccalà* (cod fillets).

Hostaria Isidoro
Via di San Giovanni in Laterano 61
☎ 06 700 8266
Closed Sat
[2]
An atmospheric place in a 16th-century convent with apparent brickwork and beautiful wall paintings. It's hard to choose between the many pasta and gnocchi dishes.

Hosteria Cannavota
Piazza San Giovanni in Laterano 20
☎ 06 7720 5007
Closed Wed
[1]
Popular with the locals: reliable cooking, generous portions and appealing if old-fashioned décor. The crayfish is worth trying.

Mario's
Piazza del Grillo 9
☎ 06 679 3725
Closed Mon
[1]
Close to Piazza Venezia, behind Foro di Augusto, a very elegant restaurant with summer terrace. Sophisticated fish dishes, carefully prepared.

TRASTEVERE

Bibli
Via dei Fienaroli 28
☎ 06 581 4534
Closed Mon lunch

An unusual combination of café, bookshop, cultural centre and Internet café.

Checco er Carrettiere
Via Benedetta 10/13
☎ 06 580 0985
[1]
At the end of Ponte Sisto, this typically Roman restaurant in an attractive old courtyard has been handed down from father to son over more than 60 years. Tasty "poor man's" cuisine using the less noble cuts of meat and offal; also fresh fish.

La Cornucopia
Piazza in Piscinula 18
☎ 06 580 0380
Closed Sun
[2]
Romantic atmosphere in this fish restaurant at the end of Ponte Palatino. In summer, you can dine outside by candlelight; inside, brick-vaulted ceiling.

Da Ivo
Via di San Francesco a Ripa 158
☎ 06 581 7082
Closed Tues
[1]
Beloved of local football fans who come to watch the matches on TV, this is a good pizzeria, with good trattoria food on the menu. In summer, the tables are set outside.

Romolo nel Giardino della Fornarina
Via Porta Settimiana 8
☎ 06 581 8284
Closed Mon
[2]
Dream setting for dinner by candlelight. The Fornarina of the name was the innkeeper's daughter, mistress of the painter Raphael.

Taverna Trilussa
Via del Politeama 23/25
☎ 06 581 8918
Open every evening
[2]
Near the Ponte Sisto, a vast choice of pasta and delectable sauces.

VATICAN AREA

L'Angoletto ai Musei
Via Leone IV 2A
☎ 06 3972 3187
Closed Tues
[1]
A friendly pizzeria near the Vatican Museums. Wide variety of toppings.

Lorodinapoli
Via Fabio Massimo 101
☎ 06 323 5790
Closed Sun
[2]
Authentic good quality Neapolitan cuisine, down to the minutest details—and not only pizzas: the menu changes nightly. A popular show-biz venue.

Piero e Francesco
Via Fabio Massimo 75–77
☎ 06 320 0444
Closed Sun
[2]
Fresh fish given the Mediterranean touch. And home-made desserts.

Zi Gaetana
Via Cola di Rienzo 263
☎ 06 321 2342
Closed Sun
[2]
Trendy, arty restaurant. "Good Food Lunch" served from 12.30 to 3pm, menu changes daily; classic dishes with unorthodox ingredients, yummy desserts.

TESTACCIO

Agustarello a Testaccio
Via G. Branca 98
☎ 06 574 6585
Closed Sun.
Reservation advised.
No credit cards.
[2]
North of Monte Testaccio near the former slaughterhouse, this is an authentic restaurant serving traditional Roman cuisine based on *quinto quarto* (fifth quarter), the part of the animal given to the workers after the saleable cuts had been removed: tongue, tail and various organs.

CityNights

The narrow streets around the Trastevere, Piazza Navona, the Pantheon and the Testaccio are the liveliest after sundown, and there are numerous nightclubs around the Via Veneto and Via Libetta (Ostiense). Concerts of sacred music held in the churches are usually of exceptional quality; programmes are posted all over town. But there's also opera and ballet, plenty to keep you entertained. To see all the possibilities Rome has to offer, consult publications such as *Città Aperta* and *Roma c'è*, the guide *Time Out Roma* (in English), or the entertainment page or weekly supplement in daily newspapers such as *Il Messaggero*, *Il Manifesto*, *Paese Sera* and *La Repubblica*.

Tickets can generally be booked online through the website of the venues, through
   www.vivaticket.it
or by calling
   Box Office, Viale Giulio Cesare 88
   Open Mon–Sat ☎ 06 3750 0375

Tickets for concerts are sold at the big music store:
   Messaggerie Musicale, Via del Corso 473
   ☎ 06 684 401

THEATRE

The English Theatre of Rome
Teatro l'Arciliuto
Piazza Montevecchio 5
nr. Piazzo Navona
☎ 06 444 1375 (office)
☎ 06686 9419
(theatre, after 4pm)
www.rometheatre.com
Founded in 1996, the English repertory theatre produces highly acclaimed plays from October to June, with one bilingual performance per season.

Teatro Nazionale
Via del Viminale 51
Box office Tues–Sat 9am–5pm, Sun 9am–1.30pm
☎ 06 481 601
Famous actors perform in contemporary plays, mostly light comedy. Also musicals and concerts. The Orchestra Regionale del Lazio performs here on Thursdays.

OPERA, BALLET

Teatro dell'Opera (Teatro Costanzi)
Piazza Beniamino Gigli 1
☎ 06 481 601
Box office open Tues–Sat 9am–5pm, Sun 9am–1.30pm, and 1 hour before performances. Students, people under 25 or over 65 qualify for

Teatro dell'Opera

half-price tickets, except on first nights. Some events are held at other venues such as the Teatro Nazionale
The Opera house has its own orchestra and ballet company. The season runs from November to May, with open-air performances in July and August in the Baths of Caracalla. Smart dress is the norm, with evening dress for first nights. Seating is mostly in boxes; you get good views from the Galleria and Balconata at the top levels where the seats are cheaper.

Teatro Olimpico
Piazza Gentile da Fabriano 17
Box office open daily (except Sun) 11am–7pm
☎ 06 326 5991
Home of the Accademia Filarmonica Romana, the theatre presents concerts, ballets and recitals of chamber music, often inviting prestigious orchestras and directors.

Terme di Caracalla
Viale delle Terme di Caracalla 52
In summer, open-air opera and ballet. Reservations at the Teatro dell'Opera. The operas are performed in the original language with Italian subtitles. You may find it useful to obtain a libretto in English when you buy your ticket.

JAZZ AND BLUES

Alexanderplatz
Via Ostia 9 (Prati)
☎ 06 3975 1877
Daily 8.30pm–3am, dinner to 10.30pm, followed by show
The oldest jazz club in Italy, with a great reputation. The most famous musicians have played here and left autographs and graffiti on the walls.

Big Mama
Vicolo San Francesco a Ripa 18
☎ 06 581 2551
Book for dinner
Tues–Sat 9pm–1.30am
Closed June–Sept
A blues heaven, but there's also jazz, played by well-known Italian and international musicians.

Classico Village
Via Libetta 3
☎ 06 5728 8857

Mon–Thurs 9pm–1.30am, Fri, Sat to 4am
In a former factory, live music, mainly jazz. DJs follow up the weekend concerts.

Fonclea
Via Crescenzio 82A (nr Castel Sant'Angelo)
☎ 06 689 6302
Open every evening
There's lots of jazz in this popular cellar club/pub, but also soul music, rock, funk, latino and R&B. Italian and Mexican food served.

Jazz and Image at the Villa Celimontana
Via della Navicella
☎ 06 589 7807
July and August
Offices Mon–Fri 9.30am–5.30pm; info tickets ☎ 06 7720 8423 from 7.30pm
Shows at 10.15pm
Programme: www.villacelimontanajazz.com
Popular jazz festival in the grounds of an ancient Roman villa, surrounded by pines, holm oaks and classical sculpture.

BARS AND CLUBS

Alpheus
Via del Commercio 36
☎ 06 574 7826
Fri–Sun 10pm–4am
Closed July and Aug
Music for all tastes, from R&B to happy trash. Live gigs, festivals, theatre and cabaret.

Il Barcone sul Tevere
Lungotevere degli Artigiani 30 (Testaccio district)
For an evening out with a difference, come dancing on a boat moored on the Tiber. Cocktail bar, disco.

Dome Rock Café
Via Domenico Fontana 18
☎ 06 705 2436
Every evening (except Mon) 9pm–2am
Trendy disco-pub, friendly atmosphere, great cocktails, electro, dark, gothic music.

Escopazzo
Via dell'Aracoeli 41
☎ 06 6920 0422
Daily 8.30pm–3am
Live music Wed–Sat, free jam sessions Sun–Tues, and a well-stocked bar where you can make your way through 200 different cocktails or excellent beers and wines (as well as food). Popular with the 30-somethings.

Gilda
Via Mario de' Fiori 97
☎ 06 678 4838
Every evening (except Mon) Restaurant and

Clubbing with Gilda

wine bar from 9.30pm, disco midnight–4am
Closed July and August when it moves to the beach at Fregene
Smart dance club for the rich and famous (jacket required).

Goa
Via Libetta 13
☎ 06 574 8277
Every night (except Mon) 11pm–4am
Ethnic disco; house, tribal, jungle, hiphop. Tuesday is gay night.

Piper Club
Via Tagliamento 9
☎ 06 855 5398
Booking advised
Famous and popular disco, music changing nightly: underground, house, rock, 70s disco. Mostly gay on Saturday.

Tartarughino
Via della Scrofa 1
☎ 06 686 4131
Dinner from 8pm, piano bar from 10pm. Closed Sun and June–Sept.
An exclusive piano bar.

ROME ON THE SCREEN

The epic scale and passionate humanity of Rome have always made it a natural for the cinema. That would have already been true if movies had existed at the time of Julius Caesar. As it was, the Eternal City had to wait till 1896 when, a few months after France's Lumière brothers had invented the cinematograph, Pope Leo XIII was filmed in the act of blessing the camera and presiding over the birth of Italian cinema. Throughout the silent-movie era, Italian cinema exploited Rome's colourful history, with patriotic themes like the birthpains of unified Italy in Filoteo Alberini's *La Presa di Roma* (*The Capture of Rome*, 1905) or the more popular blood and thunder of Julius Caesar's assassination, Nero fiddling while Rome burned and the lechery of Messalina, wife of Emperor Claudius. It's not surprising to find five films from 1912 to 1940 about the Renaissance romps and poisonous mayhem of Lucrezia and Cesare Borgia.

Cinecittà

One of Mussolini's few positive contributions to Italian culture in the 1930s—displaying his acute understanding of cinema's propaganda value—was his creation in Rome of the Cinecittà studios, together with a school for experimental cinema *(Centro Sperimentale di Cinematografia)*. The studios turned out 300 films in the first six years. Among the more celebrated alumni who made their name after World War II were directors Rossellini, Federico Fellini and Michelangelo Antonioni. The film Rossellini made in 1944 with jeeps and tanks rumbling through the bombed streets was *Roma Città Aperta (Open City)*, portraying Rome under the German Occupation, with the magnificent Anna Magnani. Several of Fellini's films were odes, bitter and sweet, to the city he loved—*La Dolce Vita* (1960) with Marcello Mastroianni fishing Anita Ekberg out of the Trevi Fountain; *Fellini Roma* (1972) with that unforgettable picture of ancient Roman frescoes erased in the light of day when uncovered by the digging of the new Metro; *Ginger e Fred* (1985), with Mastroianni again and Fellini's wife Giulietta Masina as aging dancers in a Roman studio preparing a trashy TV show.

Director Ettore Scola brought an uncompromising social view of Rome's realities with his moving saga of 30 years following the war, *C'eravamo Tanto Amati* (*They all loved each other so much*, 1974), starring Vittorio Gassman and Nino Manfredi; *Brutti, Sporchi e Cattivi* (*Ugly, Dirty and Bad*, 1976), Manfredi again in a gruesomely cynical vision of the city's shantytown suburbs; and *Una Giornata Particolare* (*A Special Day*), the poetic tale of tenement life in Mussolini's Rome, with Mastroianni and Sophia Loren.

Hollywood in Rome

Ancient Rome has provided spectacular epics such as Peter Ustinov's splendid Nero quivering in *Quo Vadis?* (1951); Marlon Brando's Mark Antony delivering the funeral oration in Joseph Mankiewicz's *Julius Caesar* (1953); Charlton Heston winning the chariot race in William Wyler's *Ben Hur* (1959); Kirk Douglas leading the slave revolt in Stanley Kubrick's *Spartacus* (1960); Anthony Hopkins doing his Hannibal Lecter number in Julie Taymor's *Titus Andronicus* (1999); Russell Crowe doing in the Emperor in Ridley Scott's *Gladiator* (2000). Hollywood has always appreciated the romantic side of Rome, too, notably with Gregory Peck and Audrey Hepburn in *Roman Holiday* (1953). Not to forget conspiracy theories of murder in the Vatican as portrayed in Francis Ford Coppola's *Godfather III* (1990).

Contemporary Rome

Today, Gabriele Muccino, a star pupil from the experimental cinema school, has moved from critical success in Rome—*L'Ultimo Bacio* (*The Last Kiss*, 2001) to box-office triumph in Hollywood, *The Pursuit of Happyness* (2006). Meanwhile, director Nanni Moretti looks at Rome with the gentle irony of *Caro Diario* (*Dear Diary*, 1993) and cynicism about Berlusconi in *Il Caimano* (*The Cayman* or *The Crocodile*, 2006).

FIAT 500

cityFacts

Airports	88
Banks	88
Climate	88
Complaints	88
Currency Exchange	88
Disabled Travellers	88
Electricity	89
Emergencies	89
Entry Regulations	90
Events	90
Horse-drawn carriages	91
Lost Property	91
Museum Passes	92
Opening Hours	92
Post Office	92
Public Holidays	93
Public Transport	93
Religious Services	94
River Cruises	94
Taxis	94
Telephone	95
Tipping	95
Tourist Offices	95

Airports
Leonardo da Vinci, or Fiumicino airport, 30 km (19 miles) southwest of the city, handles scheduled flights. It has two terminals, one for domestic and the other for international flights. Fiumicino is linked to Termini railway station (one train per hour, journey takes 30 min) and Tiburtina station (trains every 20 min; journey 40 min).

Ciampino, 15 km (9 miles) southeast of the city, is used by most charter companies.

Banks
Opening hours are Monday to Friday 8.30am until 1.20pm. The larger branches are also open from 2.30 to 4pm, but these hours may vary.

Climate
Summer, from mid-June to September, is usually very hot and stuffy. Winters are cool and often rainy. Spring and autumn are comfortably mild.

Complaints
If you have a problem in a restaurant or a shop, it's best to deal directly with the manager or the proprietor. Serious matters can be taken to the Ufficio Stranieri, Via Genova 2, ☎ 06 468 629 87, open 24 hours a day.

The price of the services of a porter or a ride in a horse-drawn taxi can always be fixed in advance. If the price of a taxi-ride seems excessive, consult the tariff which is posted inside the vehicle, not forgetting all the appropriate supplements for night service, public holidays, Sundays, and so on.

Currency Exchange
At arrival points and all over the city in front of banks and post offices there are automatic exchange machines, with instructions in several languages. Exchange offices *(cambio)* keep the same opening hours as banks. The exchange rate varies from place to place.

Disabled travellers
Rome was not built for wheelchair travel. However, there is a growing awareness of access problems, and care is taken to incorporate ramps in

new buildings and in the renovation of old ones. But the pavements (sidewalks) have high kerbs and generally lack ramps, the paving is often damaged, construction sites block the path, narrow streets do not have pavements and are bumpy, several bridges are blocked at each end by a barricade that will only allow pedestrians to pass. Metro Linea B is supposedly wheel-chair accessible, but the stations Circo Massimo, Colosseo and Cavour do not have the facilities. Modern trams have an access ramp; as for taxis, book by phone and tell the operator you have a wheelchair *(sedia a rotelle)*. You will find some information in English on the ATAC website: www.atac.roma.it ☏ 06 4695 4001, or hotline 800 154 451. To avoid too much travel in public transport, make sure your hotel is centrally located. The Roman disability organization CO.IN works to improve access in Rome and Lazio. The website has some information in English and a list of weblinks that you may find useful: www.coinsociale.it, or www.handyturismo.it which has an English version.

Electricity
Standard current is 220V, 50 Hz AC. You will need an adaptor for continental two-pin sockets.

Emergencies
Police (carabinieri): ☏ 112
Police (municipal): ☏ 113
Fire brigade: ☏ 115
Samaritani (first aid) ☏ 118
Ambulance: ☏ 06 5510 or 06 2430 2222
First aid: ☏ 06 7045 4445
Help for tourists (Pronto intervento per turisti):
　　　　　　　　　　☏ 06 6710 5228
Duty pharmacies ☏ 06 228 941
24-hour service: **Gellini**, Corso Italia 100, ☏ 06 4424 9750
Internazionale, Piazza Barberini 49,
☏ 06 482 5456
Risorgimento, Piazza Risorgimento 44,,
☏ 06 3973 8166

| Hospitals: | **Ospedale G. Eastman** (dental care), Viale Regina Elena 287B, ☎ 06 844 8312 **Policlinico Umberto I**, Viale del Policlinico 155 ☎ 06 49 971 |

Entry Regulations
You will need a valid passport to enter Italy, or, if you are a citizen of an EC country, a National Identity Card. Visas are required only for stays of more than 90 days.

Events

January	A toy market is held on January 6 in the Piazza Navona to celebrate Befana (Epiphany) personified by a witch on a broomstick, La Befana, who leaves sweets for the children.
March–April	Good Friday at the Colosseum; Via Crucis (the Way of the Cross) led by the Pope; Easter: Easter *urbi et orbi* blessing in St Peter's Square. On the Trinità dei Monti steps: azaleas and street concerts.
April–May	Painting exhibitions on Via Margutta.
May	Antiques Fair on Via dei Coronari.
June	Corpus Domini at Genzano and Castelli Romani; the streets are strewn with flowers. The festival of Saint John in the Piazza di Porta San Giovanni, roast pork *(porchetta)*, snails and fire works.
June–July	RomaEuropa at the Villa Medici; films, dance, theatre and concerts. Expo Tevere along the Tiber; an arts and crafts market, food and wine, music and fireworks.
July	Festa de Noantri at Trastevere, processions and general rejoicing.

July–August	Arte all'aperto with opera, concerts, comedy and film at the Baths of Caracalla, at Villa Ada, Ostia Antica, by the Tiber and in the parks.
	Top designer fashion shows at Trinità dei Monti.
August	Festa della Madonna della Neve at Santa Maria Maggiore, where the legendary 4th-century fall of snow is recreated in a shower of flower petals.
September–October	A craft exhibition on Via dell'Orso, near Piazza Navona.
October	Wine Festival at Marino, tastings and entertainment with wine gushing from the fountain in the main square.
	An antiques exhibition in Via dei Coronari.
December	The Festa della Madonna Immacolata in Piazza di Spagna.
	Nativity scenes in the churches, and a life-size one in St Peter's Square.
	New Year's Eve is celebrated with fireworks.

Horse-drawn Carriages

There's nothing like a tour in a *carrozzella* for getting your bearings. You can hire one for half-an-hour or for a whole day, but agree on the price with the driver before setting out. These carriages wait at Piazza di Spagna, Colosseo, Fontana di Trevi, San Pietro, Via Veneto, Villa Borghese, Piazza Venezia and Piazza Navona.

Information and reservations:
☎ 06 8530 1758   ilsogno@romeguide.it

Lost Property

If you have left something on the underground, call ☎ 06 487 4309 if it was on Line A; 06 5753 2264 for Line B.

The Lost and Found office at Termini Station has closed down because it was submerged with more "found" objects than it could handle, and which few people came to reclaim. So it's best to make sure you have all your belongings with you when you get off the train.

Museum Passes

At the tourist offices (see p. 95) you can obtain a **Biglietto 4 Musei** for €7, for the national museums (Palazzo Altemps, Palazzo Massimo, Terme di Diocleziano and Crypta Balbi). The **Roma Archeologia Card**, €20 covers the national museums mentioned above, as well as the Colosseum, Palatino Museum, Terme di Caracalla, Tomb of Cecilia Metella and Villa dei Quintili. The **Capitolini Card**, €8.50, allows entry to the Capitoline Museums (except for temporary exhibitions), and the Centrale Montemartini, Via Ostiense 106. The **Appia Antica Card**, €7, covers the Terme di Caracalla, Tomb of Cecilia Metella and the Villa dei Quintili. Each card is valid for 7 successive days and allows one single entry per sight. Reduced prices for EU citizens between 18 and 25, and for teachers.

Opening Hours

Museum opening hours are extremely unreliable. In summer, the big museums open late in the evening, sometimes until 11.45 p.m. It is best to check with the tourist office, APT. Most of them close on Jan 1, May 1 and Dec 25, and open only to 2pm on Dec 24 and 31.

Churches are generally open from 8.30 or 9am until noon or 1pm, and from 3.30 or 4pm until 5 or 6.30pm. But some can only be visited during Mass.

Shops are usually open from Monday afternoon to Saturday 9am to 1pm and 3.30 to 7.30pm (in summer, from 4 to 8pm). A few shops stay open non-stop from 10.30am to 7.30pm, even on Sunday.

In August the city is practically deserted, as it's holiday time for the Romans, including the shopkeepers. Even the nightclubs close down and head for the nearest beach.

Post Office

The Italian post office deals with mail, money transfers and telegrams. Stamps *(francobolli)* are also sold at tobacconists and often in hotels.

In the city centre, the post offices on Piazza di San Silvestro 19, at Via di Porta Angelica 23, Via Marmorata 4 and Viale Mazzini 101 generally open Mon–Fri 8.30am–6.30pm, Sat 8.30am–1pm. There are also offices at Termini Station and Fiumicino Airport.

Public Holidays

January 1	*Capodanno*	New Year
January 6	*Epifania (Befana)*	Epiphany
April 25	*Festa della Liberazione*	Liberation Day
May 1	*Festa del Lavoro*	Labour Day
June 2	*Festa della Repubblica*	Republic Day
August 15	*Ferragosto*	Assumption
November 1	*Ognissanti*	All Saints' Day
December 8	*Immacolata Concezione*	Immaculate Conception
December 25	*Natale*	Christmas Day
December 26	*Santo Stefano*	St Stephen's Day
Moveable	*Lunedì di Pasqua*	Easter Monday

Public Transport

Rome is served by orange buses, a few trams and an electric minibus, no. 119, which covers the historic centre. For a 2-hour tour of the city, take bus no. 110 from Termini Station, Piazza dei Cinquecento, daily, every 10 min, 8.40am–7.40pm. Day tickets €16. The Archeobus, leaving Piazza dei Cinquecento, daily 9am–4pm, takes you to Via Appia Antica. Day tickets €13. Combined 2-day ticket for both, €24; discount on all tickets if you book through www.trambus.com/servizituristici.htm. ☎ 06 684 0901 or 800 281 281.

The yellow Roma Cristiana bus takes two different routes past some 20 Christian sights. Leaving from Piazza dei Cinquecento, it runs daily every 30 min from 8.30am–7.30pm; audioguides, €13, ☎ 06 698 961.

The Rome underground, run by COTRAL, has only two lines:

A (orange) Battistini–Anagnina   **B** (blue) Rebibbia–Laurentina.

Certain stops are close to major monuments: the Musei Vaticani, San Pietro, Piazza di Spagna, Piazza Barberini, Termini Station, Colosseum, Circo Massimo. Trains run every 8 minutes from 5.30am to 11.30pm, and every 30 minutes during the night. Tickets are sold in the underground stations, at bus terminals, in bars and at tobacconists and newspaper kiosks. Tickets for surface transport (BIT) are valid for 75 minutes and cost €1: you can change lines with the same ticket. Underground tickets are valid for only one journey. A day ticket, BIG, costs €4. A weekly card (CIS) is available for

€16 and a 3-day tourist card (BTI) €11. To validate the ticket, enter the bus at the back and punch the ticket in the machine. If you have a day or week pass, you can enter at the front.

Religious Services

Mass is celebrated in Italian in more than 300 Catholic churches all around the city, as well as in other languages. There are churches of many other denominations, a synagogue and a mosque.

All Saints Church (Anglican), Via del Babuino 153
☎ 06 3600 1881

St Andrew's Church (Presbyterian Church of Scotland)
Via XX Settembre 7, ☎ 06 482 7627

Church of Santa Susanna (American Catholic community),
Via XX Settembre 15, ☎ 06 4201 4554

Rome Baptist Church
Piazza San Lorenzo in Lucina 35, ☎ 06 687 6652

Methodist Church Ponte Sant'Angelo
Via del Banco di Spirito 3, ☎ 06 689 6981

St Patrick's Church (Irish National Catholic Church)
Via Piemonte 60, ☎ 06 4203 1201

St Paul's Within the Walls (American Episcopal Church)
Via Napoli 58, ☎ 06 488 3339

Comunità Ebraica (Synagogue, services in Hebrew)
Lungotevere Cenci, ☎ 06 684 0061

Grand Mosque and Islamic Cultural Centre
Viale della Moschea, ☎ 06 808 2258

River Cruises

A cruise along the Tiber is a great way to see the city. Choose between a 70-min commented excursion, or 2 h 15 min dinner or winebar cruises. Departures from Ponte S. Angelo. Reservation required.
☎ 06 9774 5498 www.rexervation.com/crociere.asp

Taxis
Cabs are yellow with an illuminated "Taxi" sign on the roof; they line up at ranks and are not obliged to stop if you hail one in the street. Avoid the pirate taxis which lurk around the monuments and stations. The tariff depends on the distance, with various supplements charged for the initial hiring fee, luggage, night service, etc. Taxi drivers expect a 10 per cent tip.
   Radio Taxi ☎ 06 66 45, 06 49 94 or 06 35 70

Telephone
The telephone boxes which are scattered throughout the city require phone cards, which can be purchased from post offices, bars, tobacconists, some newspaper kiosks, the headquarters of Italian telecommunications and railway stations. Before first use, tear off the corner.
   Directory inquiries ☎ 1240
   The outgoing international code is 00. Then dial the country code (UK 44; USA and Canada 1) and the area code without the initial zero, followed by the local number.

Tipping
Service is included in the bill in restaurants, but you can always leave a few extra coins. It is normal to tip your hotel porter and anyone who carries out a personal service.

Tourist Offices
Maps, brochures and museum passes are available from the following offices:
   APT (Azienda di Promozione Turistica), Via Parigi 11, ☎ 06 488 991
   Centro Visitatori (Visitor Centre), Via Parigi 5, Piazza della Repubblica Mon–Sat 9am–7pm

The green kiosks all over town and at Fiumicino airport, Punti Informativi Turistici (PIT), are run by the municipality and provide information in several languages. Daily 9am–6pm, www.romaturismo.com

   ENIT (Italian Tourist Office) Via Marghera 2–6, ☎ 06 49 711

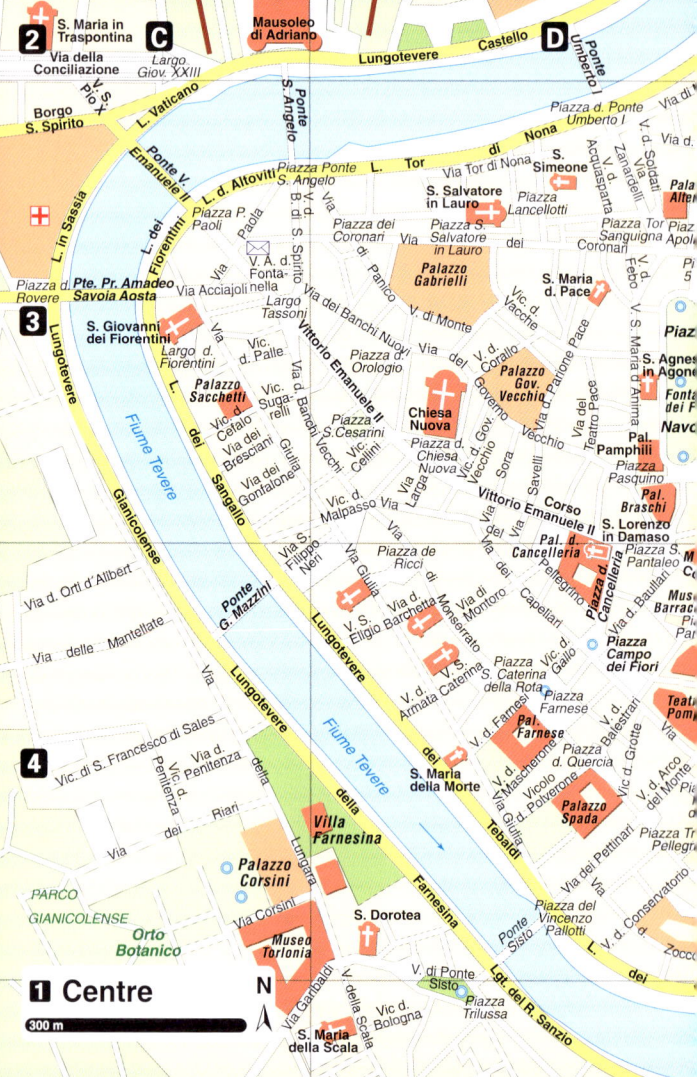

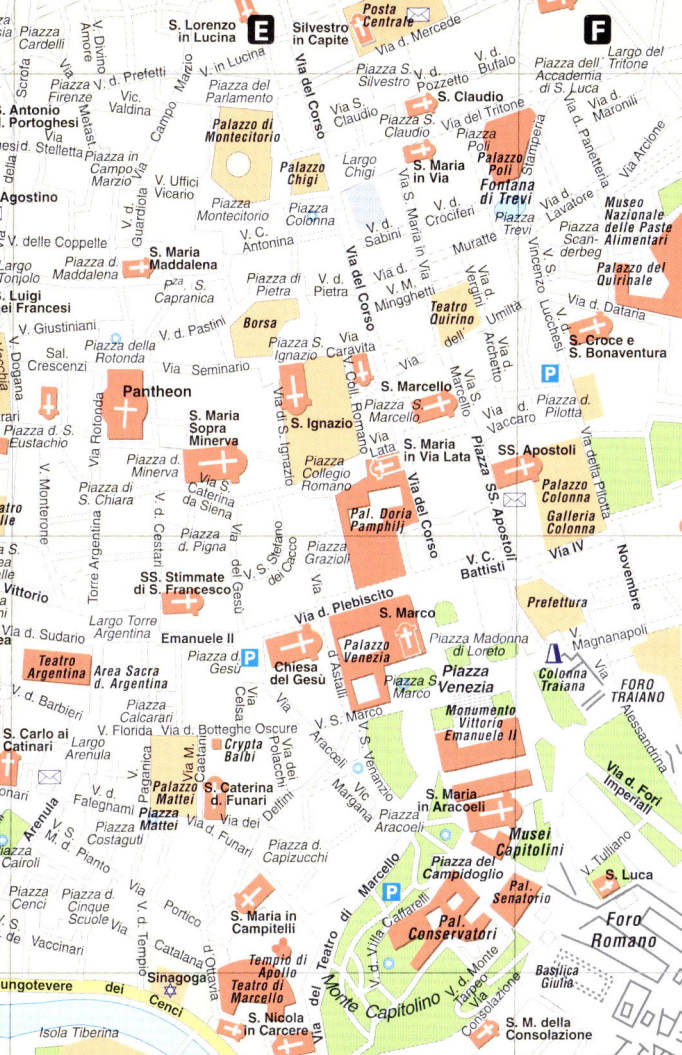

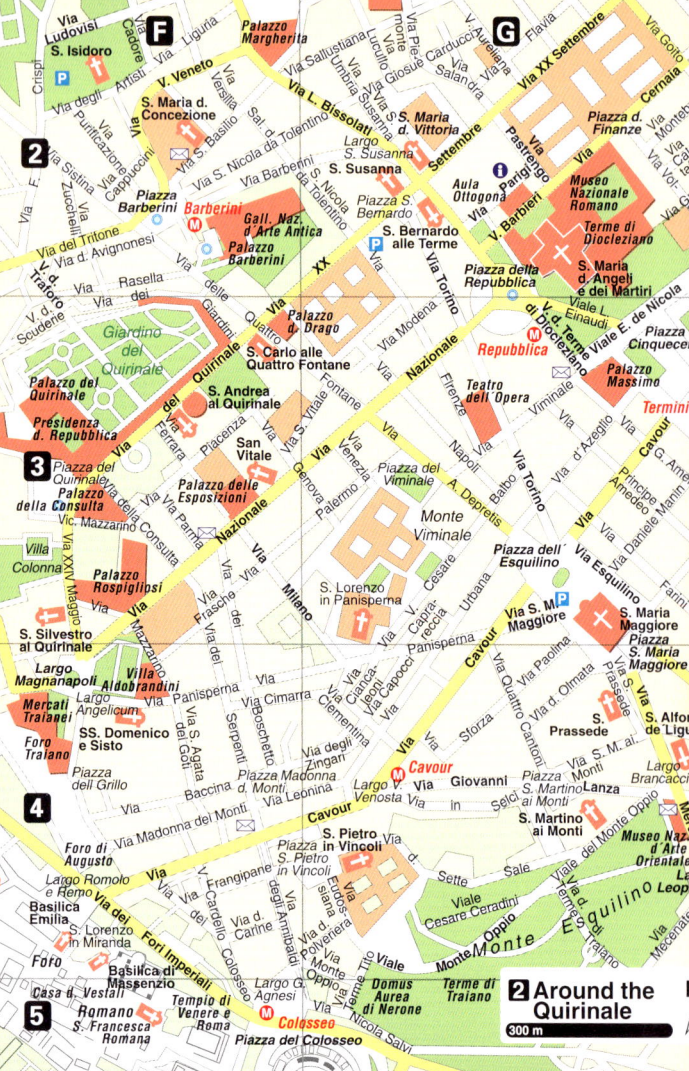

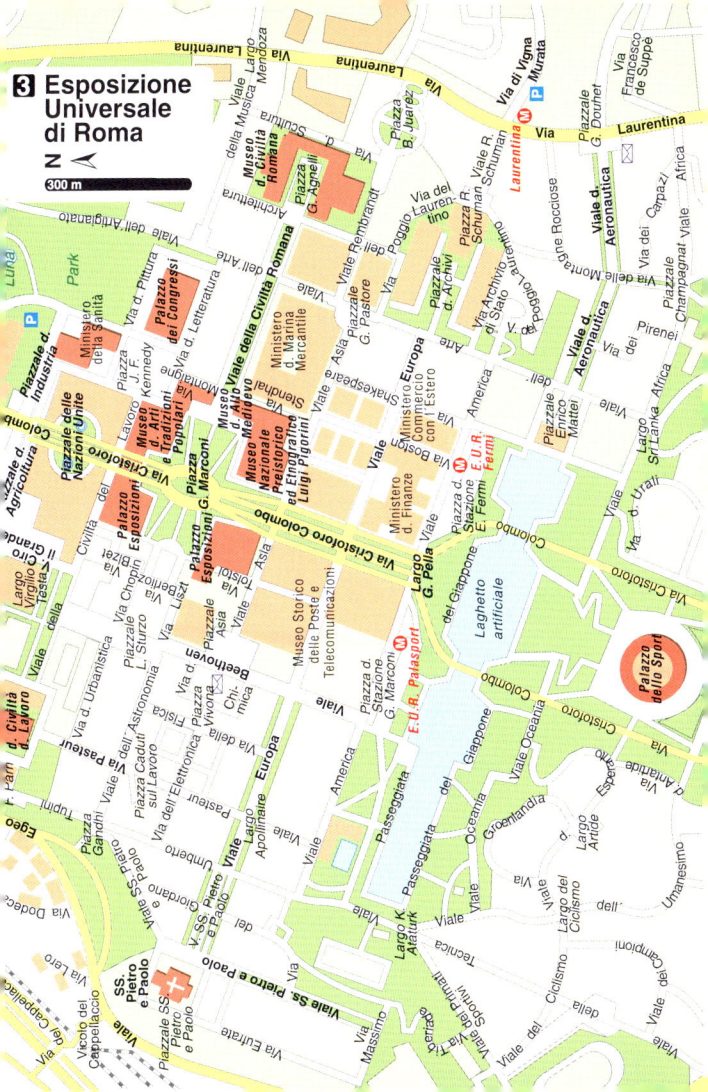

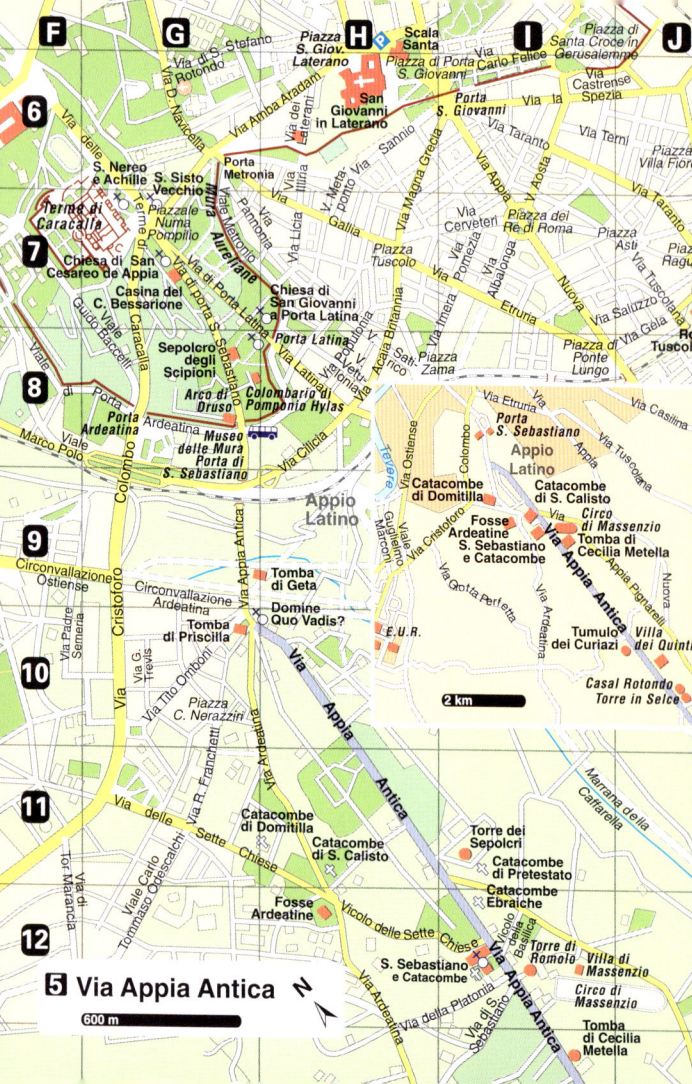

INDEX

All Saints Church 44
Appartamenti Borgia 62
Arco di Costantino 22
– di Settimio Severo 26
– di Tito 26
Art Center Acea 67
Babington's Tea Rooms 44
Basilica Emilia 26
– Giulia 26
– di Massenzio 26
Biblioteca Apostolica 62
Bocca della Verità 21, 71
Boncompagni Cerasi 44
– Sterbini 44
Caffè Canova 44
– Ciampini 44
– Rosati 44
Campo dei Fiori 35, 41
Cappella del Beato
  Angelico 62
– Sistina 61–62
Case romane del Celio 24
Casino Valadier 44
Castel Sant'Angelo 58–59, 64
Castelli Romani 68
Catacombe 25
Centro Commerciale
  Cinecittà Due 41
Chiesa del Gesù 36
– della Immacolata
  Concezione 71
Cimitero Acattolico 66
Circo Massimo 21
Civitavecchia 69
COIN 41
Collezione d'Arte Religiosa
  Moderna 62
Colonna di Foca 26
– di Marco Aurelio 30
– Traiana 19–20
Colosseo 21–22, 71
Corsia Sistina 64
Crypta Balbi 36
Curia 26
Domus Aurea 22–23
EUR 68
Explora 70–71
Farnesi Gardens 21
Fontana dell'Acqua Paola 55

– delle Api 46
– della Barcaccia 44
– del Moro 53
– di Monte Cavallo 50
– dei Quattro Fiumi 53
– delle Tartarughe 35–36
– di Trevi 30, 50
– del Tritone 46, 50
Fori Imperiali 20
Foro Romano 20
Fregene 68
Galleria Colonna 36
– Corsini 54
– Doria Pamphilj 36
– Naz. d'Arte Antica 54
– Naz. d'Arte Antica di
  Palazzo Barberini 46–47
– Naz. d'Arte Moderna 43
Galleria Sciarra 50
– Spada 35
Giardini del Pincio 42, 44
– di Villa Aldobrandini 48
– di Villa Borghese 42
Giardino del Quirinale 50
Hadrian's Villa 69
Hôtel de Russie 44
I Granai 41
John Cabot University 56
La Rinascente 41
Lungotevere Farnesina 56
Mercato dei Fiori 41
– delle Stampe 41
– di Testaccio 41
Monte Palatino 20
Monumento Vittorio
  Emanuele II 36
Mura Aureliane 24–25
Musei Capitolini 18–19
– Vaticani 60–63
Museo dell'Ara Pacis 30
– dell'Arte Sanitaria 64
– Barracco 34
– Borghese 42
– della Civiltà romana 68
– Criminologico di Roma 71
– Naz. delle Arti e
  Tradizioni Popolari 68
– Naz. Etrusco di
  Villa Giulia 43
– Naz. Luigi Pigorini 68

– Naz. di Palazzo Venezia 36
– Naz. delle Paste
  Alimentari 48
– di Roma in Trastevere 56
Necropoli dell'Autoparco 63
Obelisco Flaminio 44
Oratorio del Santissimo
  Crocifisso 50
Orti Farnesiani 21
Orto Botanico 56
Ospedale di Santo Spirito
  in Sassia 64
Ostia Antica 69
Painters 57
Palazzo Altemps 32
– Barberini 50, 52
– Buonaparte 38
– del Commendatore 64
– Corsini 56
– Doria Pamphilj 38
– Farnese 35
– Madama 31, 38
– Massimo alle Terme 52
– Mattei di Grove 35
– di Montecitorio 30–31, 52
– dei Penitenzieri 64
– del Quirinale 50, 52
– della Sapienza 38
– Testa-Piccolomini 50
– Torlonia 64
Pantheon 31, 38
Parco del Celio 24
– del Gianicolo 55, 70
Piazza Barberini 46, 50
– del Campidoglio 18
– dei Cavalieri di Malta 21
– dei Cinquecento 49
– del Collegio Romano 38
– Mattei 35
– della Minerva 52
– Navona 33, 38, 53
– del Popolo 28–29, 44
– del Quirinale 49
– della Repubblica 49
– della Rotonda 38
– San Pietro 53, 59–60, 64
– Sant'Eustachio 38
– Sant'Ignazio 38
– di Spagna 30, 40, 44

- Vittorio Emanuele II 41
Pinacoteca 63
Ponte Sant'Angelo 53, 58
– Sisto 56
Porta Portese 41
– Santo Spirito 64
– Settimiana 56
Portico degli Dei Consenti 26
Pulcino della Minerva 31
Rostri 26
San Carlino 50
San Carlo ai Catinari 35
– alle Quattro Fontane 47
San Clemente 23
San Crisogono 56
San Giovanni in Laterano 23–24
San Lorenzo in Miranda 26
San Luigi dei Francesi 32, 38
San Paolo fuori le Mura 67
San Pietro in Montorio 55
– in Vaticano 60
– in Vincoli 23
Sant'Agnese in Agone 33
Sant'Andrea al Quirinale 47, 50, 52
– della Valle 34
Sant'Atanasio 44
Sant'Ivo alla Sapienza 31, 38
Santa Cecilia in Trastevere 55
Santa Francesca Romana 26
Santa Maria degli Angeli e dei Martiri 49
– Annunziata 64
– Antiqua 26
– Maggiore 48
– dei Miracoli 44
– in Montesanto 44
– della Pace 32
– del Popolo 29, 44
– in Traspontina 64
– in Trastevere 55
– della Vittoria 52
Santa Prassede 48
Santa Sabina 21
Stanze di Raffaello 63
Swiss Guard 61
Tempio di Antonino e Faustina 25
– dei Castori 26
– del Divo Romolo 26
– di Saturno 26

– di Vespasiano 26
– di Vesta 26
Terme di Caracalla 24
– di Diocleziano 49
Testaccio 66–67
Tivoli 69
Torre degli Anguillara 56
Trinità dei Monti 44
Vatican 58–63
– Museums 60–63
Via Appia Antica 25
– del Babuino 29, 40, 44
– Bocca di Leone 40
– Borgognona 40
– della Conciliazione 64
– del Corso 38
– Frattina 40
– Margutta 44
– Sannio 41
Villa Adriana 69
– Borghese 70
– d'Este 69
– Farnesina 54, 56
– Gregoriana 69
– Medici 44
– dei Quintili 25

General Editor Barbara Ender
Features Jack Altman
Research Francesca Grazzi, Ilaria Ventresca
Cover Design Jérôme Curchod www.thebonusroom.com
Layout Matias Jolliet
Maps Elsner & Schichor; JPM Publications
Photo credits
hemis.fr/Gardel pp. 4, 72; /Frances: pp. 12 (right), 29, 47; /Mattes pp. 16, 67, 71;
/Boisberranger pp. 40, 80; David Cretegny pp. 8, 22, 41, 59
istockphoto.com/Adrian Beesley p. 12 (left); /lullabi p. 15; /Marc Schwanebeck p. 19;
/fotoVoyager pp. 33, 43, 55; /Bruce Bean p. 52; /vulkanino p. 53; winterwitch p. 70
Barbara Ender p. 37; Andreas Uebelhart pp. 61, 86;
©CinecittaStudios p.84; Corbis/cinemaphoto p. 85

Copyright © 2008 JPM Publications S.A., 12, avenue William-Fraisse, 1006 Lausanne, Switzerland
information@jpmguides.com – www.jpmguides.com

All rights reserved. No part of this book may be reproduced or transmitted in any form or by any means, electronic or mechanical, including photocopying, recording or by any information storage and retrieval system without permission in writing from the publisher.

Every care has been taken to verify the information in the guide, but neither the publisher nor his client can accept responsibility for any errors that may have occurred. If you spot an inaccuracy or a serious omission, please let us know.

Printed in Switzerland – 12033.00.2793, Weber/Bienne – **Edition 2008**

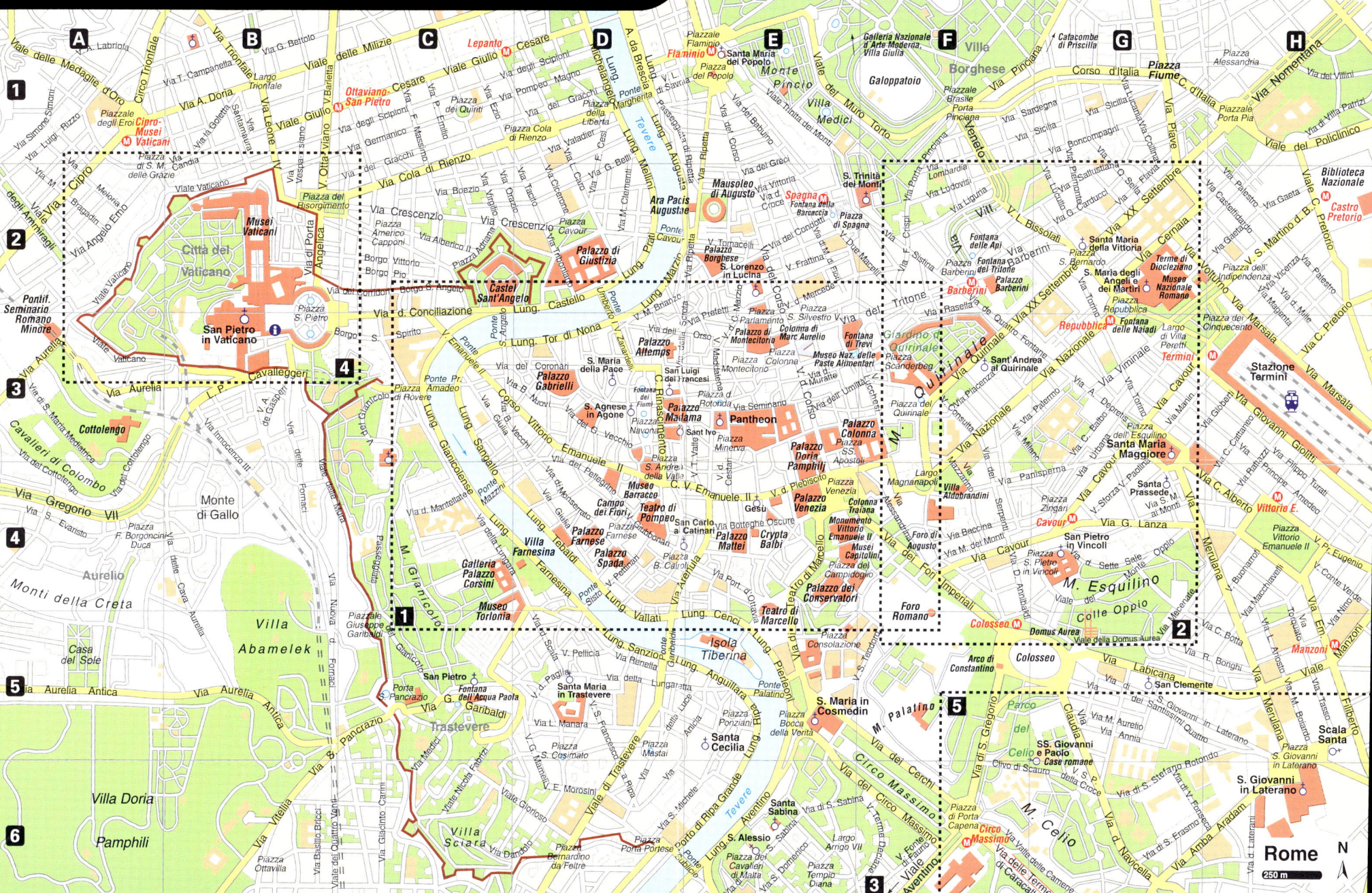